THE CELL BLOCK PRESENTS...

RAW LAW

FOR PRISONERS

MIKE ENEMIGO & KING GURU

Published by: THE CELL BLOCK™

THE CELL BLOCK
P.O. Box 1025
Rancho Cordova, CA 95741

Facebook.com/thecellblock.net

Copyright© 2019 By Wilberto Belardo

Cover design by Mike Enemigo

Send comments, reviews, or other business
inquiries:
thecellblock.net@mail.com
Visit our website: thecellblock.net

CONTENTS

INTRO

Welcome to another TCB Production! For those of you who are loyal purchasers of The Cell Block products, I can promise you that this book will pay for itself, on top of making you a profit, just like every other project you've experienced with us thus far.

Raw Law is an instructional manual on how to write and submit lawsuits while you're in prison. A Section 1983 suit is a constitutional law which is over 100 years old. This particular law created a right for every person who is in the United States to be able to sue state employees. This is the lawsuit you can use to get your point across when your constitutional rights are violated while you're locked up.

For those of you who are familiar with my individual work (How to Hustle and Win: Sex, Money, Murder Edition; How to Write Urban Novels for Money & Fame Prisoner Edition; Underworld Zilla; Pretty Girls Love Bad Boys: The Prisoners Guide to Getting Girls!), my writing style will come as a fresh breeze... easy like a Sunday afternoon. I write like I speak so my message can be easily understood by beginners as well as experts.

As you move thru these pages, you'll notice that I will emphasize the fact that your letters to the courts and legal motions don't need a bunch of complicated ten-syllable words. All those Latin and Greek words lawyers use are there to confuse and intimidate laymen writ writers. They aren't necessary. Sure, there are terms you will need to learn (if you don't already know them), but I think that after reading this book and utilizing your common sense -- you will have a working knowledge of the vocabulary needed to understand most of the legal mumbo jumbo you'll be faced with while filing these motions.

Now... I know there are those of you who will be experiencing The Cell Block for the first time. If I had to give you one piece of wisdom that will help you understand our movement it's that Mike Enemigo has recruited convict hustlers from across the country who have mastered the art of getting paid from the inside of their (our) maximum security prison cells. The Cell Block offers books like The Millionaire Prisoner; Get Out, Get Rich: How to Get Paid LEGALLY When You Get Out of Prison; CEO Manual: How To Start a Business When You Get Out of Prison!; and many, many, more. We really get bread from in here, and what makes it so proper is the fact that it's all LEGAL!

The fact that we're revolutionary in our approach to our confinement attracts haters by the horde. This is a very important aspect of the Game that you'll need to understand as you move forward on this lawsuit trip.

Section 1983 suits are used for basically two reasons: Getting money and/or stopping prison staff from doing something specific. Things understood need not be said, but I'll say it anyway... Prison staff won't be happy once you start pushing paperwork on 'em. In essence, the moment you start filing grievances, them boyz are gonna start kicking in your door. What this means is, when you make the conscious decision to become a writ writer, you're going to have to keep your cell clean from contraband. This means giving up your fuck-books, shanks, and wine making. As long as you're filing lawsuits, you'll have to be a model prisoner. Real talk.

In order for you to get into the courts you will have had to exhaust all of your institutional remedies. This means you're gonna have to take all the steps that your prison requires in the grievance system they have set up. You need to start from the bottom and reach the top. Once you've used up all your avenues through the prison grievance system, then you'll be able to file the motions that are in this book. But, that's the catch... while you're filing these complaints at the institutional level, you're gonna be open to harassment, so you gotta be prepared. You should actually welcome it because you'll be able to sue 'em for harassment, too, but we'll get to that later.

Throughout this book you'll read/see a bunch of cases where inmates across the country have sued and won thousands, sometimes millions of dollars. The reason I've added these stories is to motivate you to keep going no matter the cost.

When I mentioned the hordes of haters that you'll be faced with while embarking on this journey, I wasn't only speaking on the K9's. Other inmates will try to implant negative thoughts in your mind. They'll make you think you're wasting your time, and the Uncle Tom's will actually accuse you of fucking up their program. You can't let that type of tricknowlcdge enter your mental. The Section 1983 suit is a surefire way of getting paid. Trust me... you'll see.

I know this book isn't the first book that explains how to file a lawsuit. To me, that's cool. I recommend that you pick up other books on this same subject so that you can obtain a full understanding of this cipher. I will also say this; no other book on the market will give it to you this raw. Most books put you through pages and chapters of useless facts that won't pertain to your mission. I jump straight into the trenches with you. I'm gonna lace you on how to start your lawsuit and who you can sue immediately! Why waste time, we're trying to get paid!?Regardless of how well you understand my instructions and are able to put your suit together, it'll always benefit you to have outside support. Outside support includes a network of family and/or friends, but that's not all I'm talking about. I also strongly recommend that you contact organizations and pro bono lawyers who are interested in helping convicts push paper. Most of the cases you'll read about throughout this book where the plaintiff (inmates) won a large sum of money were only possible because of the lawyers who stepped out the shadows to help. Keep that in mind when you're campaigning for assistance.

With all of that said and done, let's get to it. Ain't nothing but to do it!

CHAPTER 1

HOW TO SET UP SHOP

Now that all the introductions are out the way it's time to get down to business... In this section I set out to break down the science on what legal motions you'll have to file to get the process started. I'm also going to explain when and where to file these motions.

First and foremost, I can't emphasize enough the fact that before any lawsuit can be filed by a state or federal prisoner, he or she MUST exhaust all administrative outlets for remedies. I'll go into it in more details shortly, but for now just know that you'll have to use your prison's grievance system before you can get this money...

Since we're already talking cash, you should know that for the lawsuits where you're seeking "MONEY DAMAGES," there is a statute of limitations. If you run out of time you'll get "time-barred." Time barred means you're case will be dismissed the moment the court sees it. Most states give you about 12 months to get it cracking, but it's always smart to find out for yourself since there are states that give you less than a year to sue for money damages.

If your mission is to change prison regulations, you're gonna need to start on this process as soon as you can. If you find yourself in a situation where a rule has been made, but hasn't been enacted yet, you really don't have to wait until it's in motion for you to start on your mission to block it. B.U.T., you do have to finish with the prison's internal grievance process before you can take it to the courts.

EXHAUSTION OF ADMINISTRATIVE REMEDIES

Let me say this again: Before you can start a lawsuit, you MUST use your prison's grievance system. You have to file at every level before you can hit the courts or your suit will get thrown out.

The actual law on it states that "No" action shall be brought with respect to prison conditions..., by a prisoner confined in any jail, prison, or other correctional facility until such administrative remedies as are available are exhausted."

Even though the term "prison conditions" sounds like things like inedible food or nasty living areas, in a case called Porter v. Nussle, 534 US 516 (2002), the Supreme Court decided that "prison conditions" refers to everything that happens in prison; which also includes police brutality and inadequate health care.

$$$$$

FEDERAL JURY AWARDS $950,000 TO PRISONERS BEATEN AT L.A. COUNTY JAIL
by Derek Gilna

Violence or the threat of violence has long been part of life for prisoners in Los Angeles County's jail system. An incident that occurred in August 2008, however, demonstrated that the most significant threat of violence comes from correctional staff. Following a contentious five-week trial, on November 7, 2013 a Los Angeles jury awarded $950,000 to five prisoners assaulted by sheriff's deputies after a protest over conditions at the jail turned violent.

Prisoners Carlos Flores and Juan Carlos Sanchez each received $200,000 in compensatory damages. Juan Trinidad received $150,000, Erick Nunez was awarded $100,000 and Heriberto Rodriguez received $90,000. The balance of the judgment, entered by the district court on February 5, 2014 was for punitive damages.

The plaintiff's attorneys conceded that approximately 30 prisoners protesting jail conditions had initially refused to comply with orders from jail staff, who were hit with debris from broken sinks and toilets. However, the attorneys argued that deputies had used excessive force to subdue the protest.

According to the lawsuit, a sheriff's captain, a lieutenant, three sergeants and 23 deputies were recorded on video hurling concussion grenades and tasering and beating prone or defenseless prisoners, causing head injuries, broken sinus bones and fractured eye sockets, legs, ankles and hands.

The plaintiff's attorneys alleged that the deputies and their supervisors had subjected prisoners to dehumanizing abuse... under color of law... [inflicting] brutal and gratuitous force that was unnecessary for any legitimate penal interest and amounted to punishment." Guards were also accused of threatening to "beat or kill Hispanic gang members" at the jail after Hispanics had allegedly killed a deputy outside his Cypress Park, California home.

At trial, deputy Nicholas Graham conceded during cross-examination that he had hit and kicked prisoners 17 to 35 times, even after they had been tasered and were lying on the floor. His own report indicated the prisoners had not been fighting back, though he still denied having used excessive force.

The jail's surveillance video footage contradicted his denial, however, despite the fact that not all of the cell extractions mandated by jail rules were available for inspection, having been inexplicably "lost."

Corrections expert Steve Martin, testifying for the plaintiffs, examined the existing videos and said the prisoners could have only engaged in "defensive or survival resistance" due to their state of restraint. The plaintiffs' attorneys alleged that "at some point during the beatings... a defendant supervisor was heard telling deputies none of the inmates should be able to walk when they left their cells."

The Los Angeles County jail employees found liable for damages in the lawsuit included Captain Daniel Cruz, Lt. Christopher Blasnek, Sgt. Micheal McGrattan, Sgt. Kelly Washington and deputies Adoph Esqueda, Mathew Thomas, Mathew Onhemus, Andrew Lyons, Michael Frazier, Blake Orlandos, Nicholas Graham, Hextor Vazquez Javier Guzman, Hernan Delgado, Justin Bravo, Francisco Alonso, Clayton Stelter, Joseph Sanford and Alejandro Hernandez Castanon.

Following the jury verdict, the district court denied the defendants' post-trial motions and they appealed to the Ninth Circuit. While their appeal was pending, on December 26, 2014 the district court awarded a total of $5,378,174.66 in attorneys' fees, with $9,500 of that amount to be paid from the plaintiffs' damage award. In November 2015 the court further awarded

$39,928.35 in nontaxable costs against the defendants. The case remains on appeal.

Additional source: www.sepr.org

$$$$$

As a rule, every grievance I write I start with the mindset that there will be a lawsuit at the end of the tunnel. Therefore, that grievance will eventually become a piece of evidence at a trial where I'm trying to get paid. That's why I always write them with as much detail as I possibly can. This includes naming each person I eventually plan to sue. The reason I name everyone is because some courts won't let you sue a defendant unless you named that person in a grievance.

When suing prison officials, you'll have to file the paperwork in the district where the incident occurred. "District Courts" are federal courts, there are 94 of them in the United States. You can find the mailing address to your local district court at your prison's law library, but I'll also include them in the back of this book.

CHAPTER 2

COMPLAINT AND SUMMONS

There's basically two motions that you'll have to draw up and submit in order to start any federal lawsuit: a "Complaint" and a "Summons." On top of that, you should also request that the court let you sue "in Forma Puaperis." This'll give you more time to pay the court's filing fee.

Damn near every single district court has a packet of forms that they'll send to prisoners (for free) so they can file actions "Pro Se" (w/out a lawyer). These forms make it easy to file, and most courts require you to use their forms anyway. To get them, all you gotta do is write a letter to the court clerk explaining that you're a prisoner and are requesting their "motion packet." I'll include addresses to the district courts at the back of this book and that'll be where you can contact their court clerks.

$$$$$

SACRAMENTO COUNTY SETTLES FORMER JAIL PRISONER'S LAWSUIT FOR $3,800

In February 2015, Sacramento County, California agreed to settle three pro se federal civil rights actions filed by a former Sacramento County jail prisoner alleging theft of his mail, opening of his legal mail outside his presence and failure to provide at least three hours of out-of-cell recreation time per week.

David Allen Thompson, Sr. was incarcerated at the Sacramento County Main Jail for 38 months. During that time, jail staff and officials with the District Attorney's Office allegedly seized his mail under false pretenses, opened his legal mail outside his presence and denied him out-of-cell recreation for up to sixty days multiple times. Sometimes Thompson received rejection notices for the confiscated mail, sometimes not. The notices he received listed the reasons for seizing his mail as "3-way mail", girls in panties, sexual content, porn photos." However, none of the letters contained any of those types of content; rather, they were often letters to and from friends or religious volunteers who visited the jail. The notices said the letters had been seized and "forwarded to the D.A.'s office."

Thompson's public defender received copies of some of the confiscated letters with the notices confirming they were being sent to a Deputy District Attorney.

Further, legal mail from courts, attorneys and government officials were allegedly delivered already opened to Thompson, though it should have been opened in his presence. When he grieved this issue, he was told the correspondence wasn't legal mail.

Thompson also received 26 disciplinary violations while at the Main Jail. During his punishment for those violations, which lasted up to 60 days, he was denied out-of-cell recreation. He complained that this violated a state statute which guaranteed a minimum of three hours out-of-cell recreation per week. The seizure of his mail and opening of his legal mail also allegedly violated state law.

Over the course of three years, from 2013 to 2015, Thompson filed three federal civil rights actions pursuant to 42 U.S.C. § 1983 against Sheriff's Department and District Attorney's Office officials alleging violations of his constitutional rights. Sacramento County settled all three suits for a total of $3,800 although $1,943.87 of that amount was used to satisfy a lien the county had against Thompson. See: Thompson v. Jones, U.S.D.C. (E.D. Cal.), Case No. 2:13-cv-01951-MCE-CKD; Thompson v. Orozco, U.S.D.C. (E.D. Cal.), Case No. 2:14-cv-02111-JAM-DAD; and Thompson v. Hones, U.S.D.C. (E.D. Cal.),

Case No. 2:15-cv-00011-TLN-DAD.

SUMMONS and COMPLAINT

To start your Section 1983 lawsuit you have to draw up and mail in two legal documents called "Summons" and "Complaint." You have to mail them to the U.S. District Courts in which whatever incidents you're suing about took place. Both of these forms will be "served" to the defendants, but all you gotta do is submit them to the courts.

THE SUMMONS

The Summons is the form that notifies the defendants that a lawsuit has been filed against them. It also lets them know about any deadlines that they have to meet before their defense is forfeited and judgement is enacted against them.

The following is a copy of what a Summons looks like:

IN THE UNITED STATES DISTRICT COURT OF WEST VIRGINIA

(Names of all the people bringing the suit.)
Civil Action No.
Plaintiff
SUMMONS

Vs.

(Names of all the people the suit is against, individually and in their official capacities.)
Defendants

TO THE ABOVE-NAMED DEFENDANTS:

You are hereby summoned and required to serve upon Plaintiffs, whose address is [your address here] an answer to the complaint which is herewith served upon you, exclusive of the day of service of this summons upon you, exclusive of the day of service, or 60 days if the U.S. Government or officer/agent thereof is a defendant. If you fail to do so, judgement by default will be taken against you for the relief demanded in the complaint.

Clerk of the court Date:

That's it! That's all you gotta draw up for a Summons. Pretty easy, huh? Now, the following is a copy of what a Complaint form looks like:

UNITED STATES DISTRICT COURT

(Names of all the people bringing the suit.)
$\qquad$ Civil Action No.
Plaintiff[s],
COMPLAINT

Vs.

(Names of all the people the suit is against, individually and in their official capacities.)
Defendant[s]

I. JURISDICTION & VENUE

1. This is a civil action authorized by 42 U.S.C. Section 1983 to redress the deprivation, under color of state law, of rights secured by the Constitution of the United States. The court has jurisdiction under 28 U.S.C. Section 1331 and 1343 (a) (3). Plaintiff seeks declaratory relief pursuant to 28 U.S.C. Section 2201 and 2202. Plaintiffs claim for injunctive relief are authorized by 28 U.S.C. Section 2283 & 2284 and Rule 65 of the Federal Rules of Civil Procedure.
2. The [name of district you're filing your suit in] is an appropriate venue under 28 U.S.C. Section 1391 (b) (2) because it's where the events giving rise to this claim occurred.

II. PLAINTIFFS

1. Plaintiff, [your full name], is and was at all times mentioned herein a prisoner of the State of [State] in the custody of the [State] Department of Corrections. He/she is currently confined in [name of prison], in [name of City and State].

III. DEFENDANTS

1. Defendant [full name of head of corrections department] is the [Director/Commissioner] of the state of [State] Department of Corrections. He is legally responsible for the overall operation of the Department and each institution under its jurisdiction, including [name of prison where Plaintiffs are confined].
2. Defendant, [warden's full name] is the [Superintendent/Warden] of [name of prison]. He is legally responsible for the operation of [name of prison] and for the welfare of all the inmates in that prison.
3. Defendant, [guard's full name] is a Corrections Officer of the [State] Department of Corrections who, at all times mentioned in this complaint, held the rank of [position of guard] and was assigned to [name of prison].
4. Each defendant is sued individually and in his [or her] official capacity. At all times mentioned in this complaint each defendant acted under the color of State law.

IV. FACTS

1. State in DETAIL all the facts that are the basis for your suit. You'll want to include what took place where, when, how, and who was there. Remember that the judge may know next to nothing about prison, so be sure to explain the terms you use. Divide your description of the facts into separate short paragraphs in a way that makes sense.
2. You'll want to include facts that you don't know personally. It can be general knowledge or it can be information given to you by people who aren't plaintiffs in your lawsuit. It's okay to include this kind of information, but you need to be sure that each time you give these kinds of facts, you have a good faith basis for believing it's true.
3. You can refer to documents, affidavits, and other materials that you've attached at the back of your complaint. Each document or group of documents should have its own letter: "Exhibit A," "Exhibit B," etc.

V. EXHAUSTION OF LEGAL REMEDIES

1. Plaintiff [name] used the prisoner grievance procedure available at [name of institution] to try and solve the problem. On [date filed grievance] plaintiff [name] presented the facts relating to this complaint. On [date got response] plaintiff [name] was sent a response saying that the grievance had been denied. On [date filed appeal] he/she appealed the denial of the grievance.

VI. LEGAL CLAIMS

1. Plaintiffs allege and incorporate by reference paragraphs 1-11 [or however many paragraphs the first four took].
2. The [state the violation.., beating, deliberate indifference to medical needs, sexual discrimination, unsafe conditions] violated plaintiff [name of plaintiffs] rights and constituted [state the constitutional right at issue, for example, cruel and unusual punishment, a due process violation] under the [state the number of the Constitutional Amendment at issue, like Eighth or Fourteenth Amendment to the United States Constitution.
3. The plaintiff has no plan, adequate or complete remedy at law to redress the wrongs described herein. Plaintiff has been and will continue to be irreparably injured by the conduct of the defendants unless this court grants the declaratory and injunctive relief which plaintiff seeks.

VII. PRAYER FOR RELEIEF WHEREFORE, plaintiff respectfully prays that this court enter judgment granting plaintiff:

1. A declaration that the acts and omissions described herein violated plaintiff's rights under the Constitution and laws of the United States.
2. A preliminary and permanent injunction ordering defendants [name of defendants] to [state what it is you want the defendants to do or stop doing].
3. Compensatory damages in the amount of $ against each defendant, jointly and separately.
4. Punitive damages in the amount of $ against each defendant.
5. A jury trial on all issues triable by jury.

6. Plaintiff's costs in this suit.
7. Any additional relief this court deems just, proper, and equitable. Dated:
8. Respectfully submitted, (Prisoner's names and addresses)

VERIFICATION

I have read the foregoing complaint and hereby verify that the matters alleged therein are true, except as to matters alleged on information and belief, and as to those. I believe them to be true. I certify under penalty of perjury that the foregoing is true and correct.

Executed at [city and State] on [date].
Signature
Type name of Plaintiff.

AMENDED COMPLAINTS

If at any point you want change your complaint, you can submit an "amended complaint." It's exactly like your first complaint, except it says "Amended Complaint" as the title. An amended complaint is basically the same complaint other than a change in a legal claim or adding or taking out some of the defendants. You might even want to change your complaint to tell the court about something that took place after you originally filed.

IN FORMA PAUPERIS PAPERS

"In Forma Pauperis," is latin for "as a poor person." Before the PLRA, inmates were allowed to file lawsuits without paying for filing or service. Now, it costs $350. However, if you're granted Forma Pauperis status, you can pay that $350 a little at a time. And if you win your lawsuits, the defendant will be ordered to pay you back!

To request this status, you'll need to file an APPLICATION TO PROCEED IN FORMA PAUPERIS. You have to request this form from the district court clerk before filing your complaint because each court has a different application.

Along with the application you'll have to file a DECLARATION in support of your application.

The clerk of courts will send you the necessary paperwork to fill out regarding your prison account. You're gonna have to file a certified copy of your prison account statement for the past six months. If you can't get a DECLARATION Form by the court's clerk, you can use the following:

IN THE UNITED STATES DISTRICT COURT
OF WEST VIRGINA

(Name of the first Plaintiff.)
Plaintiff,

Vs.

DECLARATION IN SUPPORT

OF MOTION TO PROCEED IN

FORMA PAUPERIS

(Name of first Defendant.)
Defendant,

I,_____ , am the Petitioner/Plaintiff in the above entitled case. In support of my motion to proceed without being required to prepay fees or costs or give security therefore, I state that because of my poverty I am unable to pay the costs of said proceeding or to give security therefore, and that I believe I am entitled to redress.

I declare that the responses which I have made below are true:

1. If you are presently employed, state the amount of your salary wage per month, and give the name and address of your employer

2. If you are not presently employed, state the date of last employment and amount of salary per month that you received and how long the employment lasted.

3. Have you received, within the last twelve months, any money from any of the following sources:
    a. Business, profession or form of self-employment?
    Yes   No
    b. Rent payments, interests or dividends?
    Yes   No
    c. Pensions, annuities, or life insurance payments?
    Yes   No
    d. Gifts or inheritances?
    Yes   No
    e. Any form of public assistance?
    Yes   No

f. Any other sources?
Yes   No

If the answer to any of the questions (a) through (f) is Yes, describe each source of money and state the amount received from each during the past months

4. Do you have any cash or money in a checking or savings account?. If the answer is Yes, state the total value owned.

5. Do you own any real estate, stock, bonds, notes, automobile, or other valuable property? If the answer is Yes, state the total value owned.

6. List the person(s) who are dependent on you for support, state your relationship to those person(s), and indicate how much you contribute toward their support at the present time.

7. If you live in a rented apartment or other rented building, state how much you pay each month for rent. Do not include rent contributed by other people.

8. State any special financial circumstances which the court should consider in this application.

I understand that a false statement or answer to any questions in this declaration will subject me to the penalties of perjury.

I declare under penalty of perjury that the foregoing is true and correct. Signed this _____day of_____ , 20

(Your signature.)
(Date of Birth)
(Social Security No.)

CHAPTER 3

REQUEST FOR APPOINTMENT OF COUNSEL

The "in Forma Pauperis" motion establishes the fact that due to your current circumstances you really don't have the ability to pay for legal fees or hire an attorney. The law on this gives District judges the ability to assign an attorney to you free of charge. And this is what they'll look for when deciding whether they should relegate an attorney to your case:

- How complicated are the legal issues?
- Does your case need investigation that you won't be able to do because of your imprisonment?
- Will expert testimony be needed?
- Can you afford an attorney?

Filing a Section 1983 suit against prison staff who have wronged you really isn't that hard. You go through the prison's grievance procedure and send the last few motions that I've listed to the District Court where the incident happened. That part of the Game is pretty cut and dry; where things start to get complicated is when the judge begins to make rulings (decisions) on requests that you or the Defendant make.

One of the first decisions the judge in your case may have to make is whether or not to give you a lawyer. If the judge doesn't want to assign you counsel, he doesn't have to. Getting a court-appointed lawyer to rep your case isn't that hard, but it will boil down to whether or not your case has merit. If the judge looks at your case and it looks weak, chances are, you won't get a "free" lawyer. On the flip side, if you get a "free" mouthpiece, your case must look good.

$$\$\$\$\$\$$

$1.35 MILLION TOTAL SETTLEMENT FOR SOUTH CAROLINA DETAINEE BEATEN BY JAIL GUARD
by David M. Reutter

Richland County, South Carolina has agreed to pay $750,000 to a pretrial detainee who was seriously injured after being beaten by a guard. The jail's private medical contractor, Correct Care Solutions (CCS), paid $600,000 to settle a separate lawsuit alleging the denial of adequate medical care for the prisoner's injuries.

Robert Sweeper III, 52, was arrested on trespassing charge after University of South Carolina police found him sleeping in the doorway to a classroom building on the frigid morning of February 7, 2012. He was booked into the Richland County jail, also known as the Alvin S. Glenn Detention Center.

Sweeper was placed in a suicide cell because he was behaving erratically and found to be mentally unstable, uncooperative, combative and incoherent. He refused a mental health evaluation and was later seen dunking his head in a toilet.

Over the next four days Sweeper's condition did not improve, yet CCS employees who were aware of his medical and mental problems failed to provide treatment or contact a doctor. Jail guard Robin Smith arrived at Sweeper's cell in the early morning hours of February 11 to search for weapons and other items he could use to harm himself.

When Sweeper failed to comply, Smith violated jail policy by entering Sweeper's cell. He then began to beat and repeatedly kick Sweeper, resulting in three broken ribs and two fractured vertebrae. Yet Sweeper was not examined or treated by CCS staff until three days later despite exhibiting serious injuries.

Dr. William Yates examined Sweeper on February 14, 2012. He checked his shoulder but failed to perform a complete physical exam. The next day, a local Department of Mental Health worker recommended that Sweeper be hospitalized.

A CCS nurse noted that "Sweeper had a dislocated shoulder, dehydration, psychosis, and unresponsiveness." Without an X-ray to confirm the dislocation, Dr. Yates attempted to reset Sweeper's shoulder. The doctor again failed to do a complete physical exam despite knowing that Sweeper had spent about eight hours in a restraining chair, suffered from dehydration and had an elevated pulse. Dr. Yates also knew Sweeper had been drinking toilet water, and although he prescribed mental health meds he did not order a psychiatric evaluation.

At about 4:15 p.m. on February 15, Sweeper's condition had deteriorated to the point that he was finally transferred to a hospital. "Upon admission, he was diagnosed with hyperthermia, traumatic pneumothorax (a collapsed lung), rhabdomyolysis, septic shock, fractured spine, deep vein thrombosis, acute renal failure, encephalopathy, and an acute injury to the right shoulder," according to the lawsuit filed against CCS.

A separate suit against Richland County was filed in state court but qualified for removal to federal court, where a jury verdict may have exceeded the $300,000 statutory cap on damages for tort claims. Despite the cap, county officials agreed to settle the case for $750,000, inclusive of attorney fees, in July 2014.

"If this were to move to federal court, we would be exposing Richland County to a multimillion dollar jury award," stated Councilman Seth Rose. "We also had to take into account we would also be spending a large amount of money in attorneys' fees defending what is basically an indefensible act by some employees."

The investigation that followed Sweeper's beating and hospitalization resulted in the termination of six guards for failing to report the abuse. Smith pleaded guilty in April 2014 to a federal charge of violating Sweeper's civil rights, and was sentenced to two years in prison.

$$\$\$\$\$\$$$

The following is a motion that you can use to request appointment of counsel. All the motions that I give you are pretty much universal, but keep in mind that you can always write the clerk of courts for the District you're in to ask for a copy of the specific form they use. Some District courts are finicky about their motions. Most of the time, this motion will come in the Pro Se packet you asked for at the beginning of the process. Nevertheless, here's a motion you can use:

IN THE UNITED STATES DISTRICT COURT OF WEST VIRGINIA

(Name of the first plaintiff.)
Plaintiffs,

Vs.

MOTION FOR

APPOINTMENT OF COUNSEL

(Name of the first defendant.)
Defendants

Pursuant to 28 U.S.C. § 1915 (e) (1) Plaintiff (or Plaintiffs moves for an order appointing counsel to represent him in this case. In support of this motion, Plaintiff states:

1. Plaintiff is unable to afford counsel. He has requested leave to proceed in Forma Pauperis.
2. Plaintiff's imprisonment will greatly limit his ability to litigate. The issues involved in this case are complex, and will require significant research and investigation. Plaintiff has limited access to the law library and limited knowledge of the law.
3. A trial in this case will likely involve conflicting testimony and counsel would better enable Plaintiff to present evidence and cross examine witnesses.
4. Plaintiff has made repeated efforts to obtain a lawyer.

WHEREFORE, Plaintiffs request that the court appoint, a member of the Bar, as counsel in this case.

Date

Signature,

Print name below

Address

DECLARATIONS

A declaration is any statement made by someone involved in your case that you'll want to use as evidence. It's a sworn statement of facts written by someone with firsthand knowledge of the "facts." Anytime you have a case with more than one Plaintiff, all of you need to make your own declaration.

A little earlier, I pointed out that in order for the judge to appoint you counsel he or she will have read your case and feel that it has some sort of merit. With that in mind you should always start every lawsuit with as much "heat" as possible. A declaration is an "exhibit" that supports your complaint. Each exhibit has its own letter, like: "Exhibit A., Exhibit B," etc. I strongly recommend that you submit as many declarations with your initial complaint as possible. It'll establish substance to your case and that's what you want. As a rule of thumb, you should always come as hard as you can as quick as you can.

You can submit a declaration anytime you want to. It doesn't have to be with your complaint. And this is cool because sometimes you don't have access to all your witnesses when you first start your lawsuit. Anytime you locate a witness who's willing to testify, draw up a declaration and send it in to the clerk of courts. Just be sure to include your CIVIL ACTION NUMBER on any paperwork you submit.

(example of a Declaration)

IN THE UNITED STATES DISTRICT COURT
FOR THE SOUTHERN DISTRICT OF
CALIFORNIA

Simmons,
Plaintiff
DECLARATION OF Al Jabar

Vs.

Dixon,
Civil Action No. 09-cv-86

Defendants

Al Jabar hereby declares:

I have been housed at Pelican Bay State Prison since 2016. Since April of 2018 I have been housed in D Facility 8 building. I am currently in cell 104, which is directly next to cell 103. Maximus Simmons is currently in cell 103, and has been for several months.

On June 30, 2009, I saw C.O. Brown approach cell 103, and enter the cell. A few minutes later, I heard a blood curdling scream along with multiple banging sounds. That's when I heard inmate Michael Simmons screaming for his life. It sounded like he was being raped.

A few days later, I noticed Warden Dixon standing in front of Simmons' cell, peering in. He stood there for close to 3 hours (without making a sound), and then left.

I declare under penalty of perjury that the foregoing is true and correct. Executed at Pelican Bay State Prison, CA on December 2, 2018.

Al Jabar

$$$$$

NEW YORK: $225,000 SETTLEMENT FOR PRISONER'S SUICIDE ATTEMPT, ABUSE AT RIKERS ISLAND

In July 2012, the City of New York paid $225,000 to settle a lawsuit that alleged 17 causes of action arising "from a chain of disturbing events" that involved the treatment of a mentally ill prisoner at Rikers Island.

When Rort Fecu was booked into the Anna Kross Center on Rikers, it was well known and documented that he had a history of mental illness, including bipolar disorder and suicide attempts prior to his incarceration. An April 15, 2009 medical screening and order by the court for a mental examination put jail staff on notice of Fecu's mental health condition.

Despite that information, on July 13, 2009, a guard accommodated Fecu's request for a razor and allowed him to use it without supervision. Fecu attempted suicide by using the razor to cut his arms "on or near the bilateral antecubital fossa."

Following a hospital stay for treatment, Fecu was housed in the Mental Health Assessment Unit for Infracted Inmates at Rikers with a September 18, 2009 directive that he be placed on suicide watch for the remainder of his time at the jail. However, his history of psychiatric problems and suicidal behavior did not result in proper care and treatment.

Fecu was denied his prescribed psychotropic medication and stopped eating on or around September 24, 2009. He went without eating through October 13, dropping from 218 to 180 pounds during that period, and jail officials allowed him to "remain without food or sustenance and medication" over that time.

On October 13, 2009 a guard once again fulfilled Fecu's request for a razor. He used the razor to again attempt suicide by slashing his arms. Fecu was returned to Rikers Island sixteen days later and placed back on his medication regimen. He overdosed on pills on November 9, 2009 but rather than treat him or otherwise limit his access to an excessive amount of pills, he was taken off his medications.

Guards came to Fecu's cell on November 15 and left him with nothing but "a bed frame, toilet and his orange jumper." The following day, several guards and "someone believed to hold the rank of Captain" entered Fecu's cell. He was pushed against a wall, put in an arm lock and stripped naked.

A guard used his arm to slam Fecu onto the bed frame and pin him there. Fecu was struck several times on the head. "While Fecu was down, one of the officers stuck their fingers up his anus," the complaint stated. The guards laughed and taunted him before leaving him "naked, dazed and bleeding."

A medical clinician saw Fecu in that condition and had him taken to the clinic. A group of guards, including those who had assaulted him, were there when he arrived. He was threatened not to report the assault and returned to his cell. The clinician again had him brought to the clinic, and he was taken to "urgent care" where he received 8-10 stitches.

Fecu was subsequently released from Rikers but incarcerated in early May 2010. Despite his past mental health history, he was placed in general population. On May 5, 2010 he attempted suicide by hanging himself with a bed sheet in his housing area's bathroom. He lost consciousness and required extensive medical treatment, but survived.

In a subsequent lawsuit against the City of New York, Fecu raised federal Constitutional and State law claims. The city's $225,000 settlement, including attorney fees and costs, was reached on July 12, 2012.

CHAPTER 4

HOW TO "SERVE" YOUR LEGAL PAPERS

Not only must you send copies of your Summons and Complaint to the judge in your case, you also have to serve both papers on all the defendants on your case. If you've never been "served" a subpoena I'm sure you've seen someone in a movie get served. It's how you let the defendants know they're getting sued.

The good and simple news is that provided you filed for and were granted the advantages of in Forma Pauperis, your complaint will automatically be served quickly and without cost by the U.S. Marshal's Service.

Another way to get out of paying a process server or U.S. Marshal to deliver your motions is by asking the defendants to waive service under Federal Rule of Civil Procedure 4(d). You do this by mailing them a request for Wavier of Service. You should be able to find these forms in your prison's law library. They're in the Federal Rule of Civil Procedures Appendix of forms, Form 1A and 1B. Save copies of both the NOTICE OF A LAWSUIT and REQUEST FOR WAIVER OF SERVICE OF SUMMONS (that is all one document).

When you send these documents to the defendants, make sure you add a copy of your complaint, a S.A.S.E., and a copy of the request. Either way, there's a chance that the defendants won't agree with your request to waive service. Nevertheless, chances are, you'll get your Forma Pauperis granted at some point, so don't think it's the end of the world if the defendants play hardball.

The good news is that the complaint and summons are the only documents that have to be served in this manner. But, just like everything else, you should always check with your specific District Court for specific rules since different districts have different rules about filing and serving documents.

$$$$$

MINNESOTA COUNTY JAIL PAYS $1 MILLION IN MEDICAL NEGLECT CASE
by Lonnie Burton

In a settlement that is believed to be the largest of its kind for a medical neglect claim in the state of Minnesota, Hennepin County agreed to pay $1 million to a mentally ill prisoner who stabbed himself in both eyes after being held in jail for 40 days without proper psychiatric care.

Michael Schuler was arrested in 2012 for missing a court date and booked into the Hennepin County jail. Schuler, who had a lengthy history of mental illness that was known to county authorities as far back as 2009, was denied his antipsychotic medications by jail medical personnel.

Jail records indicated that Schuler had a history of numerous drug overdoses, self-inflicted stab wounds and chronic suicidal ideations. He was previously hospitalized eight times in Hennepin County.

In addition to denying Schuler his antipsychotic medications, jail staff meticulously chronicled his steady mental deterioration and the minimal treatment he received.

Prior to his arrest for missing a court hearing, Schuler was hospitalized at the Hennepin County Medical Center's psychiatric unit. Doctors recommended that he remain at the Medical Center because he was a danger to himself and others; however, administrators overruled the doctors and Schuler was discharged. As he was leaving the hospital, he was arrested for the missed court date and taken to jail. Records indicated the only reason Schuler had missed the court date was because he was hospitalized at the time.

After 40 days in the county jail with no medication or treatment, Schuler used a pencil to stab himself in both eyes [See: PLN, Nov. 2013, p.281]. He is now blind in his right eye and has severely impaired sight in the left. Jail records showed that Schuler complained of mounting anxiety and repeatedly asked for his medications, which were withheld at one point due to his "behavior issues."

By the time Schuler was released from the hospital following treatment for his eyes, his medical bills totaled over $400,000.

Hennepin County Sheriff Richard Stanek, who in 2013 played a lead role in successfully lobbying the Minnesota legislature for a law that requires mentally ill prisoners to be placed in a state mental health facility within 48 hours after being committed by a judge, decline to comment on the case.

Schuler was represented by attorneys Robert Bennett and Andrew Noel of Minneapolis, and

William Lubov of Golden Valley, Minnesota. See: Schuler v. Otterblad, U.S.D.C. (D. Minn.), Case No. 0:13-cv-01151-SRN-TNL.

According to a news report published by the Star Tribune, on a typical day the Hennepin County jail holds between 100 to 200 prisoners with serious psychiatric disorders, often one-quarter of the facility's total population. The new law aims to reduce that number, but beds at the hospital's psychiatric unit are in short supply.

$$$$$

Another note to remember: Be sure to keep a personal copy of everything you send the courts. You never know when something will get "lost" in the mail. If you don't have access to a copying machine, make copies by hand. If your situation is really grimy, send copies to your people on the streets. However you gotta do it, always have a copy of all your paperwork where you can gain access to 'em easily.

CHAPTER 5

STRUCTURING YOUR LAWSUIT

To be a TCB writer you gotta be a businessman above all else, yet everyone on the line-up is a convict... including myself. Needless to say, we're for the "people," we're for the "movement," and definitely for the notion that being a convicted felon who's sentenced to a prison term does not forfeit the natural right that we all have to be treated and respected as men. So, yes, I recommend to anyone using this book that you utilize the knowledge within it to make these modern-day slave traders pay you cash. Yet, I also understand that it's not always all about money. There are times in life when you're gonna have to stand up for something, and that's what this chapter is all about.

The United States Constitution guarantees all Americans certain rights. Yeah, getting convicted of certain crimes will get some of your rights taken away. Things like the right to buy guns, vote in elections, and/or travelling out of town can be restricted or taken away. You can even get snatched up and placed on a modern- day slave plantation. But, the truth of the matter is that no matter what crimes you've been convicted of, these folks still gotta treat you like a man.

I've done state time in several different states, so I've seen and experienced oppression at its worse. The worst place I've done time was in the state of Florida. Doing time in California is so different that guys on the West Coast sometimes don't believe the stories I tell them. I've done time at FSP, Santa Rosa C.I., and Charlotte C.I. I know what it feels like to be beaten while shackled. I know what it feels like to get pepper sprayed for doing nothing more than looking out the window of my cell door.

If you're in a situation where you see or experience oppression and/or police brutality, you CAN change it. You CAN fight it, but you gotta use their tools to battle them in their arena. Instead of waging a war you can't win (violence), pick up that pen and file on they ass!

$$$$$

NEW YORK SETTLES WRONGFUL CONVICTION CLAIM FOR $2.7 MILLION
by Michael Brodheim

In November 2012, the State of New York agreed to pay $2.7 million to settle a claim filed by a woman who was wrongfully convicted and imprisoned for over 13 years.

Lynn DeJac was convicted in April 1994 of the second-degree murder of her 13-year-old daughter, Crystallynn Girard, who was found naked in her bed at their Buffalo home. An autopsy reported that she had been strangled and had non-lethal levels of cocaine in her system.

DeJac, who had been drinking and arguing with her boyfriend, Dennis Donohue, the night before Crystallynn's death, was convicted despite the absence of any physical evidence. In exchange for the dismissal of unrelated felony charges, DeJac's friend, Wayne Hudson, falsely testified that she had confessed to him that she killed her daughter. Sentenced to a term of 25 years to life, DeJac steadfastly maintained her innocence.

In 2007, the cold case squad of the Buffalo Police Department took a second look at the evidence in Crystallynn's death. They discovered similarities with two other murders that were linked to Donohue, one involving a woman who was strangled.

Police had found blood on the shirt that Donohue wore on the night that Crystallynn died in but it was not tested at the time. He had no alibi for that night, and had been implicated in stalking DeJac after she ended their relationship.

The cold case examination revolved around the presence of Donohue's DNA at the scene of Crystallynn's death, as well as inside her vagina. Based on these findings, DeJac's conviction was vacated on November 28, 2007 and she was released from prison.

A subsequent re-examination of the autopsy records led to a determination that Crystallynn had died due to a cocaine overdose and not from strangulation; the original autopsy was in error.

Donohue had provided grand jury testimony implicating DeJac after being granted transactional immunity by prosecutors. Thus, he could not be charged in connection with Crystallynn's death, though he was later convicted of murder in another case and sentenced to 25 years.

In 2008, within months of being cleared of criminal wrongdoing, DeJac, who married and changed her name to Peters, filed a claim against the State of New York pursuant to § 8-b of the Court of Claims Act, seeking damages for her wrongful conviction and imprisonment. Four years later she accepted the state's settlement offer $2.7 million.

Although cleared in her daughter's death, DeJac never received a public acknowledgement of her innocence from law enforcement. To the contrary, according to a federal lawsuit that she filed against Buffalo Officials, Joseph Marusak, the Assistant District Attorney for Erie County at the time of DeJac's prosecution, continued to insist that she had murdered Crystallynn. The suit accuses Marusak of participating in a conspiracy to deprive DeJac of her civil rights and seeks $10 million in damages.

Unfortunately, DeJac did not live to see an end to the lawsuit or enjoy her settlement for long; diagnosed with cancer in 2013, she died on June 18, 2014. She was 50 years old.

Her suit against the Buffalo Police Department and individual defendants, including police detectives, remains pending on behalf of her estate.
See: Peters v. City of Buffalo, U.S.D.C. (W.D.N.Y.), Case No. 1:10-cv-009553-WMS-JJM.

$$$$$

The following 3 options are called "relief."

- MONEY DAMAGES: It's when the court orders the defendants to break you off some cash to make up for their actions.

- DECLARATORY JUDGMENT: When a court makes a decision that breaks down your legal rights and the legal duties and obligations of the prison officials it's called a declaratory judgment. Nevertheless, even though a judge is documenting your rights in a declaratory judgment it isn't actually telling the prison to stop what they're doing. At that point, it's on them to follow the law on their own.

- INJUNCTION: This is when the court actually orders the defendants make changes at the prison, or stop their on-going conduct. A court will usually only issue an injunction when it feels that money won't be enough. And they will most likely issue a declaratory judgment and an injunction together. Yet, it is possible that a judge will issue a declaratory judgment alone so the prison will be able to come up with their own remedy.

MONEY DAMAGES

There are three types of money damages. The first one is called "nominal damages." Nominal damages are small amounts like $1.00. Yeah, this is the type of award you'll get when you can prove that your rights were violated, yet the actual harm committed was so diminutive that it can't be compensated.

The second type of money damages is called "compensatory damages." This is when officials pay you for medical and other expenses, for any wages you lost, for the value of any part of your body or physical functioning which can't be replaced or restored, and for your pain and suffering. In these cases you'll get a significant amount of money.

Punitive damages. To get punitive damages, the officials had to either hurt you on purpose, or do something so obviously dangerous, they had to have known it was likely to hurt you. The key is to show that the defendant's actions were "motivated by evil motive or intent" or involved "reckless or callous indifference to your rights."

Not all punitive damage awards require physical assault. The point of punitive damages is to punish members of the prison staff who violate your rights and to set an example to stop other prison staff from acting illegally in the future.

[NOTE:
A. You can get nominal damages if your rights have been violated.
B. You can get compensatory damages to make up for physical or other harm you were caused.
C. You can get punitive damages to punish guards who hurt you on purpose.]

INJUNCTIONS

The courts can actually order the prison staff to stop or change any action that is found to be harmful to inmates. It doesn't matter whether they've doing it for five days or five decades, if it's violating your constitutional rights and you can prove it, the judge can make 'em stop.

An injunction is the order issued by a court that tells the defendant to do or not do something. If the defendants don't follow the court's order, they can be held in "contempt" by the court that issued the injunction. This means someone will be fined or put in jail.

You're only gonna be able to get an injunction if you can show the court that the defendant's actions show "actual or imminent injury." In other words, you gotta show that you're being harmed in some way, or that you likely will be soon.

You can't get an injunction for something that already happened, but might not happen again. For instance, if a guard beat you up for getting smart with him, you're better off asking for money. Now... if guards routinely beat up inmates for not cleaning up their cell, then that's something where an injunction would work perfectly.

There are two different kinds of injunctions. Permanent Injunctions and Preliminary Injunction. The first one happens after a trial where the courts decided one was necessary (after the first two years of a permanent injunction, defendants can challenge it every year). A preliminary injunction is what you can get during the trial. You can ask for it during the court procedure if your life is in danger or rights are being continuously violated.

There are four things you have to show in order to receive a preliminary injunction:

1. That it will serve the public interest.

2. The threat of harm for you is greater than the harm the prison officials will face if you get a preliminary injunction.

3. You're likely to receive an injury that can never be fixed (irreparable harm).

4. When it's obvious that you're gonna win at trial.

Here's a copy of the actual motion you can use:

IN THE UNITED STATES DISTRICT COURT
FOR THE

(Name of the first plaintiff on the case.)
ORDER TO SHOW CAUSE

Plaintiffs,
FOR A PRELIMINARY INJUNCTION &

TEMPORARY RESTRAINING ORDER

Vs.

(Names of first defendant on the case.)
Civil Action No.
Defendants

Upon the complaint, the supporting affidavits of plaintiffs, and the memorandum of law submitted herewith, it is:

ORDERED that defendants [names of defendants against who you are seeking a preliminary injunction] show cause in room of the United States Courthouse, [address] on the day of [month], [day], [time], why a preliminary injunction should not issue pursuant to Rule 65(a) of the Federal Rules of Civil Procedure enjoining the defendants, their successors in office, agents and employees and all other persons acting in concert and participation with them, from [state the actions you want the permanent injunction to cover].

IT IS FURTHER ORDERED that effective immediately, and pending the hearing and determination of this order to show cause, the defendants [names of defendants whom you want temporary relief] and each of their officers, agents employers and all persons acting in concert or participation with them, are restrained from [state the actions you want the TRO to cover].

IT IS FURTHER ORDERED that the order to show cause, and all other papers attached to this application, be served on the aforesaid Defendants by [date].

Judge's Signature
Dated

UNITED STATES DISTRICT JUDGE

$$$$$

The reason this form has so many blank spaces is because it's an order for a judge to sign. All you're doing is writing it for the judge. He/she will fill in the blanks when the time comes.

The hardest part of the form to fill out will be the section where you have to explain why you want the TRO. Try to limit it to the things you want the prison officials to stop immediately.

[Preliminary Injunctions are only good for 90 days at a time.]

CHAPTER 6

INITIAL RESPONSE TO YOUR COMPLAINT

This section covers what happens right after your suit is filed and served. This is when problems with your complaint are gonna be raised, either, by the District Court or by the defendants in a motion to dismiss. This is also when you need to be on point, since you're gonna have to defend your complaint against the motion to dismiss, or it'll be time to reshape/correct any errors that are brought to your attention.

$$$$$

NEW YORK PRISONER'S RETALIATION CLAIM NETS $147,000 IN DAMAGES, FEES AND COSTS
by David Reutter

A New York federal jury entered a verdict that awarded a state prisoner $40,002 in a case alleging a First Amendment retaliation claim, and post-trial the court awarded over $107,000 in attorney fees and costs.

New York prisoner Juna Hernandez initiated a pro se civil rights action against "no less than twenty-three employees of two New York State Department of Corrections and Community Supervision" facilities where he had been incarcerated. Over the course of the litigation he was granted leave to amend his complaint three times.

Hernandez was appointed counsel in September 2013, and the case proceeded to a six-day trial in May 2014. The jury found the defendant not liable on an Eighth Amendment excessive force claim against four guards, but found guard Darren Williams and prison counselor Robert Smith had retaliated against Hernandez for filing grievances and the instant lawsuit.

The jury awarded Hernandez $1.00 each in nominal damages against Williams and Smith; it also awarded $25,000 and $15,000 in punitive damages against Williams and Smith, respectively. Following the verdict, both Hernandez and Williams filed post-trial motions.

The district court reviewed the motions and granted Hernandez leave to amend his complaint to include facts about an incident upon which the jury had entered its liability finding against Williams; the court found no prejudice accrued due to Hernandez giving "longstanding notice" during discovery that the incident was part of his retaliation claim.

The district court dismissed as untimely Williams' motion for judgment as a matter of law, then turned to Hernandez's motion to award attorney fees and costs. The court held counsel was entitled to $165 per hour for services prior to March 1, 2014 and $189 per hour after that date. It applied those rates to the 364 hours of work reasonably performed, resulting in a $60,003 attorney fee award plus $47,103.99 in costs.

The district court required Hernandez to pay $2,000 of the attorney fee award from the jury's verdict, and ordered Williams to pay $36,251.51 of the fee award and Smith to pay the remaining $21,751.49 They were held "jointly and severally liable for the costs." See: Hernandez v. Goord, U.S.D.C. (S.D. NY), Case No. 1:01-cv-09585-SHS; 2014 U.S. Dist. Lexis 113720.

A. INITIAL PROCESSING

Once your complaint is filed, the clerk's office is gonna assign a Civil Action Number to your case. This'll be like a social security number to your case. You need to make sure it's on every legal document you file.

The clerk's office will also assign your case to a district Judge and a Magistrate, and they might ask you which one you prefer. If both you and your opponents consent, the Magistrate judge will act just like a district judge in your case and issue a final ruling, which you or your opponents have the option to appeal like any other judgement.

Before you make the decision as to whether, or not, you'll go with a Magistrate over the district judge, you should do everything in your power to find out as much as you can about both of 'em: Which one knows more about inmate rights? Whose caseload is heavier? Who's more willing to help Pro Se litigants? It could be as easy as flipping a coin, but then again, you should always try to tip the scales of justice in your favor.

B. DISTRICT COURT SCREENING

Right after the clerk's office processes your complaint, it's the district courts job to "screen it." The PRISON LITIGATION REFORM ACT (PLRA) requires courts to dismiss any lawsuit that is:

1. "Frivolous or malicious."
2. Fails to state a claim upon which relief may be granted.
3. Seeks money damages from a defendant who is "immune" from damages liability.

If a district court dismisses part or your entire lawsuit during the screening process and you believe it's a bad call, you need to get on that real quick! You'll have to file OBJECTIONS to the judge's recommendation. It has to happen within ten days, and if that's denied, your only option will be an appeal (& you'll only have 30 days to do that...).

C. WAIVERS OF REPLY

Based on the PLRA, defendants have a third option in ways of a reply (On top of the traditional two: 1. Motion to Dismiss 2. Motion to Answer.) They can file a "Waiver of Reply." Basically what this means is they can choose not to reply at all! As long as they don't reply-- the courts can't grant any relief.

Don't trip, though. If whomever you're suing files a waiver of reply, the district court has to review your suit to see if you have "a reasonable opportunity to prevail on merits." And this process isn't that much different than the first level of screening. So, if you made it through the initial screening-- they'll most likely order them to reply.

Now, if they still attempt to refuse to reply, you can file a motion on "default judgement." Under

Federal Rule of Civil Procedure 55 we have several different procedures for requesting default judgements, depending on the kind of relief you want and the defendants you're suing. Just for the record, courts don't like to grant it, they'll most likely just force 'em to respond.

D. DISMISSAL MOTIONS

Once your complaint gets past the initial screening process, the defendants must file either a motion to dismiss or an answer. If your suit names multiple parties or asks for different forms of relief, the defendants can file for a FULL DISMISSAL (challenging your entire lawsuit) or PARTIAL DISMISSAL (challenging only some of your claims).

If the court grants the motion, your lawsuit will end at the district court level. If the judge denies the motion to dismiss, the defendants will have 10 days to reply. Even a full dismissal can be appealed though, so, even if the motion to be dismissed is granted-- don't ever give up!

GROUNDS FOR DISMISSAL

A. Rule 12 (b) (1) Grounds

ELEVENTH AMENDMENT: The Eleventh Amendment to the U.S. Constitution bars § 1983 lawsuits against states and state agencies. However, the Eleventh Amendment does not bar lawsuits (1) against state officials in their individual capacity for damages or (2) against state officials in their official capacity for injunctive relief.

LEGISLATIVE, PROSECUTORIAL, AND JUDICIAL IMMUNITY: Legislators, prosecutors and judges are almost always shielded from liability.

FAILURE TO EXHAUST ADMINISTRATIVE REMEDIES: Thanks to the Clintons, the Prison Litigation Reform Act prohibits inmates from filing federal lawsuits until you complete all available administrative remedies. If you don't go through all the grievances and appeals at the prison-- you can't sue!

PHYSICAL INJURY REQUIREMENT: The Prison Litigation Reform Act bars inmates from seeking damages for "mental or emotional" injuries if they didn't suffer related physical injuries too.

RES JUDICATA AND COLLATERAL ESTOPPEL:"RES JUDICATA" is claim preclusion: A party may not file a new lawsuit if an earlier lawsuit involving the same parties and the same cause of action ended in a final judgement.

"COLLATERAL ESTOPPEL" is issue preclusion: A party may not re-argue a factual issue that was litigated and decided in an earlier lawsuit or criminal case involving that party.

$$$$$

NINTH CIRCUIT UPHOLDS $106,000 IN DAMAGES PLUS ATTORNEY FEES FOR WITHHELD EVIDENCE
by Mark Wilson

The Ninth Circuit Court of Appeals has upheld a $106,000 damage award and over $348,300 in attorney fees and costs for an innocent man's 27-month pretrial confinement after two police detectives' knowingly concealed compelling evidence of his innocence.

Between June 27 and August 15, 2005, Los Angeles Police Department detectives Robert Pulido and Steven Moody investigated thirteen "demand notice" robberies. By the sixth robbery they believed a single suspect was committing the crimes. One of the robberies occurred at EB Games on August 13, 2005.

When Michael Walker entered EB Games three days later, he was arrested because a store employee thought he looked like the man who had robbed the store.

Walker, a homeless ex-felon, professed his innocence. He consented to a search of an apartment where he stored his belongings, and no evidence on any robbery was discovered. His fingerprints did not match those found at the crime scene. Nevertheless, Moody and Pulido concluded that Walker had committed all thirteen robberies.

Within days of Walker's arrest, while he was in custody, the demand note robberies continued. The suspect's description matched that of the suspect who had committed the other, earlier robberies.

Moody was "surprised" to hear about the continued robberies and immediately assumed the same suspect had committed all of them. He shared this theory with Pulido.

Stanley Smith was arrested after fleeing from a September 15, 2005 demand note robbery, and the robbery spree ended with his arrest. Regardless, Moody and Pulido did not alert the prosecutors in Walker's case that the demand note robberies had continued after Walker was in custody. Rather, following Smith's arrest, Moody wrote two reports for prosecutors in September and November 2005, falsely declaring in bold print: "Since the arrest of Walker the crime spree caused by the 'Demand Note Robber' has ceased." Pulido approved both reports.

In mid-2007, Walker's attorneys finally learned about the robberies that Smith had committed. A demand note recovered at the scene of one of Smith's robberies shared an identical misspelling with a note in one of the robberies that Walker had been charged with, threatening that the perpetrator would "start shooting."

On November 26, 2007, Walker's attorneys alerted prosecutors of Smith's arrest and noted that Smith's fingerprints were found at the scene of the EB Games robbery attributed to Walker. Walker's case was dismissed the same day, ending his 27-month pretrial confinement. The trial court later entered a finding of factual innocence.

Walker filed a federal lawsuit against Moody and Pulido in 2008, alleging they had violated his constitutional rights by concealing material exculpatory evidence. The case went to trial and a jury returned a verdict for Walker, finding that Pulido and Moody failed to disclose compelling exculpatory evidence to the prosecutor and did so with deliberate indifference to, or reckless disregard for, the truth and Walker's rights. The jury awarded $106,000 in compensatory damages.

The district court then denied the defendants' motion for judgment as a matter of law and awarded Walker $336,948 in attorney fees and $11,382.24 in costs. Moody and Pulido appealed. The Human Rights Defense Center joined the National Police Accountability Project of the National Lawyers Guild in a letter to the Ninth Circuit in support of Walker's position on appeal.

The appellate court affirmed on September 17, 2014. Moody and Pulido "affirmatively misrepresented -- twice -- highly material facts," the Court of Appeals found. Further, they did not "correct the misinformation provided to the prosecutors, or provide accurate information concerning Smith's arrest and the consequent end of the [robbery] crime spree, during the two year period Walker remained in pretrial detention."

A police officer's continuing obligation to disclose highly exculpatory evidence to the prosecutors to whom they report is widely recognized," the Court added. However, it also emphasized "the narrowness of the constitutional rule we enforce today, which is restricted to detentions of (1) unusual length, (2) caused by the investigating officers' failure to disclose highly significant exculpatory evidence to prosecutors, and (3) due to conduct that is culpable in that the officers understood the risks to the plaintiff's rights from withholding the information or were completely indifferent to those risks."

The Ninth Circuit further affirmed the attorney fee and cost award, noting that "Moody and Pulido's appeal from the award of attorney's fees is contingent upon their appeal of the judgment. They have not brought a particularized challenge to the calculation of the attorney's fees awarded... or alleged an abuse of discretion."

See: Tatum v. Moody, 768 F.3d 806 (9th Cir. 2014).

$$$$$

B. Rule 12 (b) (1) Grounds

FAILURE TO ALLEGE ELEMENTS: This law allows the judge to throw your case out if it failed to state a relief that can be granted. This rule attacks the lack of details. You can't claim that C.O.'s knew you were in danger if you can prove that they had deliberate indifference, because deliberate indifference is a lot more than mere negligence.

DEFENDANT'S INVOLVEMENT: The courts can dismiss your complaint if you fail to give details on why you're adding each defendant to it. And, remember, a defendant can be liable even if she wasn't at the specific incident your complaint revolves around. For example, a Captain can be responsible for a constitutional violation if he tells staff to make the dormitories so cold that the inmates won't want to get out of bed. Even though he may not have turned the heat down and air up, he's still responsible.

QUALIFIED IMMUNITY: This shields officials from damages liability if existing case law didn't "clearly establish" the right that they allegedly violated. Defendants can only use this if you are suing them in their official capacity. Everything that was agreed upon, and what wasn't. After the court receives the Rule 26 report, it'll enter a scheduling order that sets the deadline for all involved parties to amend their pleadings, file motions, and complete discovery.

AUTOMATIC DISCOVERY: Federal Rules require each party to produce certain information even if no one asks for it. Whoever fails to comply with automatic disclosure is subject to sanctions, including banning them from using undisclosed evidence later.

The first two provisions of Rule 26 (a) (1) cover a lot of ground. Disclosure (A) tells both parties to list the name, address and telephone number of everyone who has information about the issues in the lawsuit. Whatever the defendants list in their disclosure will be a good starting point for your discovery efforts. Disclosure (B) tells all parties to produce copies of "all documents, data compilations, and tangible things in the possession, custody, or control of the party" that are relevant to disputed issues and will be used to support its defense.

If you're seeking damages, Disclosure (C) requires you to give a computation of all the category of damages you're asking for, along with any documents or evidentiary materials on which your computation is based. You should include medical records, proof of lost wages, etc...

By far, you're gonna have a lot more to gain from initial disclosures than the people you're suing. In Disclosure (A), list everyone you can think of who has information about your lawsuit; inmates, guards, medical officials, family members. For Disclosure (B), provide copies of all relevant documents you have.

30 days before trial, FEDERAL RULE OF CIVIL PROCEDURE 26 (A) (3) requires all parties to disclose the names, addresses, and telephone numbers of witnesses whom the party will call to testify.

And, everyone has a duty to supplement an automatic disclosure or discovery reply if the party learns that the disclosure or response "is in some material respect incomplete or incorrect and... the additional or corrective information hasn't otherwise been made known to the other parties during the discovery process or in writing."

So, if any new information has been found by any party involved, throughout the discovery process it's on them or you to let the other know what you found.

$$$$$

TENNESSEE PRISONER AWARDED $60,000 FOR GUARD'S USE OF EXCESSIVE FORCE

A Tennessee federal jury awarded $60,000 to a prisoner after finding three guards at the Riverbend Maximum Security Institution (RMSI) in Nashville had used excessive force.

The verdict found that prison guards Joshua McCall, Gaelen Doss and Sean Stewart used excessive force on former prisoner Todd Lee White while he was held in a segregation unit at RMSI. The incident occurred on May 31, 2010 -- Memorial Day.

Because White and other prisoners in the unit were in segregation, they were confined to their cells 23 hours a day and received showers only on Monday, Wednesday and Friday. McCall said there would be no showers that day because the unit was on "holiday schedule."

Prisoners began banging on their cell doors, but McCall reiterated there would be no showers. When a nurse came to the cell of prisoner Ryan Honeycutt, he threw liquid on a guard. A short time later, guards arrived at Honeycutt's cell, handcuffed him, Beat him, broke his nose and left him without medical care.

About an hour later, guards returned to the unit to pass out dinner. When they approached White's cell, he told the guards he knew what had happened to Honeycutt and said the incident should be reported to the shift commander. He then threw a milk carton full of cold coffee and water on the guards.

Four guards, including McCall, came to White's cell about 30 minutes later and ordered him to submit to handcuffing. McCall said he must not have seen what they did to Honeycutt. White responded that he had, and demanded that the shift commander show up with a video camera before he would submit to handcuffing, as he was in fear for his safety.

The guards left and returned with other RMSI guards in riot gear. Lt. Bryan Baldwin assured White he would not be beaten, and directed him to face the wall with his hands behind his back and get on his knees. Once White did so, guards entered the cell with an electric shield and shocked him; they then commenced to kick, hit and beat him. White was placed in handcuffs and shackles, and a guard hit him in the eye, knocking him "unconscious for some period of time." He awoke to more blows, and knees on his back. Once pulled to a standing position, a blow to his head caused a split in his forehead from the top of his hairline to between the eyebrows.

Finally, Lt. Baldwin said, "that was enough, bring him out of the cell." White was carried down a staircase and slammed on the floor at the bottom. He was dragged to a recreation area, but his injuries resulted in such severe bleeding that a nurse was called. White was taken to a hospital where "approximately ten to fifteen staples" and other sutures were needed to close his wounds.

At trial, the guards pointed fingers at each other. They acknowledged the force used was unnecessary, but no one took responsibility. While McCall denied using excessive force himself, he blamed Doss and Stewart. Doss admitted to an internal investigator that he had used excessive force but denied it at trial.

The jurors made a culpability statement with their verdict: They awarded White $30,000 in compensatory damages against McCall and $15,000 each against Doss and Stewart.

The district court entered the judgment on January 21, 2015; costs of $4,482.65 were taxed against the defendants, and on August 31, 2015 the court awarded $82,257.90 in attorney fees. White was represented by attorneys David L. Cooper, Blair P. Durham and Benjamin E. Winters.

$$$$$

DISCOVERY TOOLS

Written questions served on other parties are called INTERROGATORIES. Parties must answer or object to each interrogatory separately and under oath. Here's the type of information you should be looking for:

- The identity of parties and their agents or employees.

- The identity of the defendant's witnesses, including any experts.

- The existence and location of documents and exhibits relevant to your claims.

- Details about particular events.

- The defendants' position about issues in the case.

Facts, exhibits, witnesses, and other evidence that the defendants plan to use in opposition to your claims.

Don't worry about the defendants answering your interrogatories because they have to.

FEDERAL RULE OF CIVIL PROCEDURE 33 requires parties to answer interrogatories within 30 days after being served. You/Them, must answer each interrogatory separately, with either an answer or an objection. If either side objects to a question, it must "state the reasons for objection and shall answer to the extent the interrogatory isn't objectionable." Documents are critical to your lawsuit.

FEDERAL RULE OF CIVIL PROCEDURE 34 allows you to serve on a defendant a REQUEST FOR THE PRODUCTION OF DOCUMENTS. This includes any or all "writings, drawings, graphs, charts, photographs, phono-records, and other data compilations from which information can be obtained." You can file a document request at any time during the discovery process, but it's better to do it early on.

FEDERAL RULE OF PROCEDURE 34 (A) also provides for (1) the inspection of tangible things in a party's possession or control, and (2) entry upon a party's land or other property "for the purpose of inspection and measuring, surveying, photographing, testing, or sampling the property or, any designated objection or operation thereon." If a particular thing or condition is in dispute in your case, consider filing a request to inspect it.

Prison officials are most likely gonna try to pump the breaks on letting you inspect their property on the ground that your request endangers security. So, you're gonna have to explain to the court how your request is reasonably calculated to lead to the discovery of admissible evidence.

RESPONDING TO DEFENDANT'S DISCOVERY REQUEST

Just like you can use the Federal Rules to discover information from the defendants, they can also flip it to get information and exhibits from you.

Always keep in mind, in these cases, it's on the plaintiff (you) to prove your case. Defendants don't have to present any evidence at all. On top of that, in these cases, defendants usually have more resources to conduct discovery than you do. So, you're gonna have to be on your toes when they get to requesting discovery and depositions.

Prepare yourself for contention interrogatories. CONTENTION INTERROGATORIES ask you to justify allegations: e.g., "State all facts which you contend support your allegation that Officer Stench Mouth put your life in danger." When responding to a question like this, make sure you write down every possible fact that supports the allegation in question. It's actually better to bombard the defendants with information than to leave an important fact out.

Expect the defendants to take your deposition. It'll most likely take place at your prison. Defendants and their lawyers can attend your deposition, but other officials can't come in. Here's some advice on how to act when you're in the "Hot-Seat."

- Listen to every question. Answer that question only, and keep your answers as short as possible. Never volunteer any information, PERIOD!

Once you answer a question:

- SHUT UP! Even if the lawyer looks at you with a stupid facial expression like he expects you to say something else.

- Never let 'em knock you off your square. Stay cool at all times. Don't let yourself get angry or upset. That's what they're paid to do, so don't slip!

- If you don't understand a question, let 'em know. Never answer a question you don't fully understand.

- Think before you speak. Don't interrupt a lawyer's question. You do have the right to object, so if a lawyer interrupts an answer you're giving -- exercise that right immediately.

- At the end of a deposition, you (as a Pro Se party) can give additional testimony.

- You should only do this if you think your earlier testimony was unclear or misrepresented.

- And, finally, you need to be careful if the defendants take your deposition. It can last for several hours and, chances are, you'll get tired and frustrated. But, you gotta be on point at all times 'cuz the defendants can use your testimony against you at a later date.

CHAPTER 7

TRIAL

If you reach this point in the Game, I tip my hat to you. In my experiences, the only time suits make it to the trial point is when the case is serious and there's big money involved. I'm also sure that if you get to this level you'll most likely have a lawyer repping you, so you'll be alright. But, that doesn't mean you shouldn't know what's going on. You should always attack every aspect of this lawsuit trip as if you're doing it yourself without representation. Especially, since there are instances where some of you will be going into these arenas on your own. So, let's get to it...

District courts like to set trial dates from the beginning of the discovery phase even though they know that date will most likely get delayed. The purpose of that is to keep all parties focused, and possibly instigating a settlement.

All before the trial, the courts will order PRETRIAL CONFERENCES to make the case run more efficiently. You'll probably attend these hearings telephonically; pay close attention! And always be ready to talk "SETTLEMENT."

Right before trial, the court will call a FINAL PRETRIAL CONFERENCE." The participants at any such convergence shall format a plan for trial, including a program for facilitating the admission of evidence.

This is called FINAL PRE-TRIAL ORDER or FPTO and it includes the following:

- Any amendments to the complaint and answer.

- For jury trials, proposed voir dire questions and jury instructions.

- For a bench trial, the requirement of when the trial brief is due.

- Statement of your case to be read to the jury.

- Statement by defendants of their case that will be read by the jury.

- The relief that the plaintiff wants.

- Facts that the parties stipulate to (agree on).

- Issue of facts and questions of law that remain to be decided at trial.

- Witnesses that each party will call.

- Exhibits that each party will call.

Before trial, you should prepare yourself to file some important motions. These are the ones right here:

- MOTION IN LIMINE: This is a request to limit the evidence that the other side may present at trial. This motion will help limit irrelevant issues the defendants are gonna try to bring up.

- RIGHT OF HABEAS CORPUS AD TESTIFICANDUM: This motion will get a court order directing prison officials to bring the inmate you want to testify to court on a specific date.

- You're also gonna have to serve WITNESS subpoenas on all of your non-inmate witnesses. And you'll be expected to pay each witness a fee and travel allowance required under 18 U.S.C. § 1821 unless you file a motion to proceed IN FORMA PAUPERIS and it's granted.

$$$$$

$750,000 SETTLEMENT IN NEW MEXICO "CONTROLLED SEATING" LAWSUIT
by Matt Clarke

In September 2013, a proposed settlement was filed in a lawsuit over forcibly seating inmates "nuts-to-butts" for hours at a time at a New Mexico state prison -- a practice also known as "controlled seating." The settlement provides $750,000 to be divided among the class members after incentive payments to the class representatives, attorney fees, expenses and the costs of administering the settlement.

The class-action lawsuit was originally two separate suits filed against prison officials, one of which was brought in state court and the other in federal court and the two cases were then consolidated.

The complaint described incidents that occurred four times at the Central New Mexico Correctional Facility in Los Lunas in 2009 and 2010 under Warden Anthony Romero, who allegedly implemented a policy of intimidation and abuse of prisoners. The specific incidents involved a practice called "nuts-to-butts" by the plaintiffs and "controlled seating" by the defendants. It involved prisoners being stripped to their boxer shorts, manhandled and thrown against a wall by masked, armed guards, then forced to sit front-to-back in a line with their legs straddling and genitals touching the buttocks of the prisoner in front of them.

Prisoners subjected to "control seating" were required to hold this humiliating position for hours, sometimes with their fingers intertwined and hands on their heads so they had to use their naked thighs to grip the prisoner in front of them to support their weight. Those who were unable or unwilling to sit "nuts-to-butts" were thrown against the wall and physically and verbally abused. Many prisoners believed they would be shot by the shotgun-carrying guards if they failed to maintain the position.

No toilet breaks were allowed and some prisoners urinated on themselves. They and the other prisoners around them were then forced to continue sitting in the pool of urine.

Warden Romero allegedly told the prisoners they were his "bitches" and that he could make them sit "nuts-to-butts" any time he wanted and would do so unless they all showed what he considered to be proper respect to his officers.

The prisoners were represented by Albuquerque attorneys Matthew Coyte and Jack Bennett Jacks, who negotiated a settlement of $750,000 for the 422 class members subjected to "controlled seating." According to the settlement agreement, the funds will be distributed as follows: $10,000 to each of the six named class representatives, $250,000 in attorney fees, $27,683.83 in costs and sales tax, and up to $20,000 for claims administration.

The remainder of the settlement is to be divided among the class members according to how many filed a claim and how many times they were subjected to "controlled seating." The minimum payment to a class member is $528.73 for one incident, $586.19 for two, $1,057.46 for three incidents and $2,114.92 for four. The defendants also agreed to change DOC policy to specify that "No inmate shall be made to sit straddling another inmate with less than approximately on foot gap between the inmates."

"We've come a long way," said Coyte. "It took two years to get to this point, in the face of denials that happened at all."

The district court granted preliminary approval of the proposed settlement in July, 2014. A fairness hearing was held on November 13, 2014, and the court entered final approval of the settlement six days later. Only one class member objected to the settlement. See: Oates v. Dorsy, U.S.D.C. (D. NM), Case No. 1:11-cv-00254-MCA-GBW.

Meanwhile, Warden Romero was promoted to Deputy Director of the New Mexico DOC's Adult Prisons Division.

$$$$$

TRIAL

Your trial is either gonna be a bench trial or a jury trial. If you ask for money damages, or you or the defendant request it, you'll be having a jury trial. After trial, the jury will decide how much damages the defendant must pay, or whether or not your rights have been violated.

At a bench trial a district judge or a magistrate decides whether your rights were violated, and whether or not you should receive damages.

As the plaintiff in a civil trial, the burden of proof is on you. It's on you to prove each element by a PROPONDERANCE OF THE EVIDENCE. What this means is that the judge or the jury must come to the conclusion that what you're claiming happened are more likely than not true. In a nutshell, you don't gotta prove your allegations without a reasonable doubt. You just gotta prove it as good as you can.

WITNESS TESTIMONY

We've all watched Law & Order on TV. Some of us have even been to trial. You already know that a large part of the actual trial is witness testimony. When you're questioning "your" witnesses, it's called DIRECT EXAMINATION. When the defendants are questioning "your" witnesses it's called CROSS EXAMINATION, and vice versa. After cross-examination, the lawyer who called the witness can ask more questions on RE-DIRECT.

When you call your witnesses to the stand you want to start with people who have firsthand knowledge of the incident. Someone who was actually there when the incident happened. The questions you ask friendly witnesses should be open-ended. What that means is a question that can be answered in a few different ways. You don't want to be seen as leading a "friendly" witness.

Of course, you're gonna know the answers to your questions, especially when dealing with friendly witnesses. But, you should still work with (in other words... coach/prepare) all your witnesses prior to trial, especially inmate witnesses. Prepare them by telling them to always speak clearly, only include relevant details, and to keep his composure at all times. The seat gets hot under cross-examination, you don't want your witness snapping on the defense, no matter how disrespectful they get.

On the flip-side, when questioning an ADVERSE WITNESS, you can/should ask leading questions. A "leading question" looks something like this:

Q: You knew on Wednesday night that my eye socket had been crushed in, right?

A: I guess...

Q:At 2:15, you did count and I was standing at my door with blood dripping down my face, didn't you?

A: Yes.

Q: I looked like I was in excruciating pain, didn't I?

A: Yes...

The defense doesn't want to answer questions that'll make 'em lose the case. But, by asking them "leading" questions, you don't give 'em a choice. This is where that lawyer's adage comes from: "Never ask a question you don't know the answer to."

Cross examination is a powerful tool. This is when you can put the defense's witnesses on the hot seat, but, then again, you can't go too hard or you run the risk of looking like a bully.

Here's a few gems to keep in mind for your cross examination tactics:

- Never ask a question you don't already know the answer to. Cross examination isn't the time to fish for new info. You should've done all that during the discovery phase of your trial.

- "Stay ready" so you don't have to "get ready." Review everything every witness has ever said, written-or signed before trial. This'll let you know what to attack and what not to ask.

- Don't try to bring up everything a witness said on direct. People have short attention spans, it's best to keep it to around three points during cross-examination.

- A way to "control" witness testimony is by asking short, leading questions. But don't ask questions that start with "why" or "how." If a person doesn't answer your question, ask it again. Don't get mad, don't let 'em play you for your cool. And, if a witness is really refusing to answer a question, ask the court to direct the witness to answer.

- If a witness testifies on direct examination in a way that's inconsistent with a statement he already made, you can work on impeaching him/her.

There are four basic ways to impeach a witness.
1. Recommit the witness to the testimony he gave on direct examination. You do this by asking the question he lied on, and getting him to lie again.

2. Introduce the liar to his prior statement. You can do this by pulling out a copy of the deposition, or whatever paperwork you got 'em talking on before.

3. Show why the first account is more likely to be true than the witness's direct testimony. This is when you use your mouthpiece. Explain your point to the judge and/or jury.

4. Confront the witness with the lie. This doesn't mean you should call 'em a liar or get loud with 'em. Just call him on it and keep it pushing. Move on to the next pint. You'll have time in your closing to speak on it again, so don't play yourself.

OBJECTIONS

If you believe a legal error has take place, or is about to happen, you can bring it to the court's attention by objecting. Objections need to be made quickly at trial. If the defense ask a witness an improper question, you need to object before the witness can answer. Even if your objection is sustained, if the jury has heard some damaging testimony you might not be able to bounce back from it.

Objections serve two purposes. (1) If the court overrules or denies a party's objection, and if that party loses at trial, it will have preserved its ability to challenge the claimed error on appeal. (2) If the court sustains the objection (rules in favor of the party making the objection), the error will be immediately corrected.

Consult the FEDERAL RULES OF EVIDENCE and a treatise on evidence or trial practice for more information on objections.

$$$$$

$2,250 JURY AWARD IN ARKANSAS PRISONER'S EXCESSIVE FORCE CASE
by Matt Clarke

In a verdict handed down on August 21, 2014, a federal jury found in favor of an Arkansas prisoner who claimed prison guards had provoked him into attacking them so they could beat him. The jury award of $2,250 included compensatory and punitive damages.

Keith Moored, a state prisoner, was incarcerated at the Grimes Unit in Newport when Sgts. James Hill and Lantz Goforth approached him, along with Sgt. Richard Lee and Cpl. Charles Poole. According to court documents, Lee told Moore that he was being placed under investigation and ordered him to turn around so he could be restrained.

Moore protested, saying he had done nothing wrong. Lee told him there was a report that he had been in a verbal altercation with another prisoner. Moore asked to speak to a higher-ranking prison official, then Lee and Goforth used a chemical agent on him.

Infuriated, Moore hit Lee in the back with his fist. In response, Hill began continuously striking Moore in the face and left side of his head. Moore was sprayed again; he dropped to his knees and then to the floor, no longer resisting.

Hill knelt atop Moore's back and started hitting him all over his body with a closed fist. With Goforth, Lee and Poole holding Moore down and preventing him from curling up on the floor, Hill continued the assault. Moore's hands were cuffed behind his back while Hill kicked him in the eye with the toe of his boot.

Moore suffered permanent damage to his left eye, rendering his vision 20/200 in that eye. He also suffered a brain contusion and injury to his right thumb. He filed a Pro Se federal civil rights action pursuant to 42 U.S.C. § 1983 against all four guards, alleging Hill and Goforth used excessive force and Goforth, Lee and Poole failed to stop Hill's use of excessive force.

A ten-man, two-woman jury took about five hours to reach a verdict. They found in Moore's favor against Hill and Goforth, while finding in favor of Lee and Poole. The jury awarded $500 in compensatory damages and $1,000 in punitive damages against Hill, and $250 in compensatory damages and $500 in punitive damages against Goforth. Both were found liable in their individual capacities.

Little Rock attorney David Hargis was appointed by the court to represent Moore pro bono. Hargis praised Moore, noting that he had won the initial part of the lawsuit on his own.

"He's a bright guy," said Hargis. "Finally, a little win in his life."

Considering the injuries that Moore received, though, it was a paltry win. The Arkansas Department of corrections took no disciplinary action against the guards. The district court denied a post-trial motion for judgment as a matter of law, and the state paid the compensatory damages in April 2015.

See: Moore v. Hill, U.S.D.c. (E.D. Ark.), case No. 5:1 2-cv-00206-DPM.

$$$$$

VERDICT OR DECISION

In a jury trial, the judge will give JURY INSTRUCTIONS after closing arguments. Jury instructions tell the jurors what law they must apply during their deliberations. Some jury instructions deal with basic issues like the plaintiff's burden of proof.

You can suggest alternative language in your objections to other proposed instructions. And you can object to any proposed instructions that state the law incorrectly or in a confusing or biased way.

In a bench trial, the judge decides the case after closing arguments. He can immediately issue his decision, or he can call a recess in order to come to a conclusion.

If you lose at the district court level, you can file an appeal by filing a NOTICE of APPEAL with the district court clerk (not the court of appeals clerk) within 30 days after the final judgment. Your notice of appeal must identify all the parties who are appealing, the judgment or order appealed from, and the court to which you're appealing.

If the district court enters a judgment directing the defendants to pay you damages, and the defendants refuse to pay, you may enforce the judgment by filing a WRIT OF EXECUTION. Defendants don't usually have to pay damages awards while they're pursuing post-trial motions. However, if they lose those motions and/or appeal, they gotta pay you interest on the award beginning from the date the district court entered judgment.

Now, if the judge grants you an injunction, and the defendants fail to comply, you can enforce the injunction through CONTEMPT PROCEEDINGS.

Here's the basics to it:

1. You file a motion for an order to "show cause" why the defendants shouldn't be held in contempt.

Support this motion with evidence, with declarations and exhibits, showing that the defendants haven't made a reasonable effort to comply with the injunction.

2. If the court enters a "show cause" order, the defendants must either show that they have made a reasonable effort to comply with the injunction.

3. The district court may conduct an evidentiary hearing to resolve any factual disputes. That's when it'll decide whether or not the defendants are in contempt.

4. If the judge holds the defendants in contempt, it will decide what, if any, contempt remedies are appropriate.

District courts have an array of tools at their disposal designed to coerce defendants into compliance and/or to compensate people who've been injured by defendants' non-compliance. One remedy they like to push is the PER DIEM fine: An order directing the defendants to pay a certain amount of money every day until they're in full compliance.

We all know the deck is stacked against us, but then again, if it were going to be easy everybody would be doing it....

CHAPTER 8

YOUR RIGHTS

When I first caught this life sentence, my sister, who had been to prison four times, told me to get my hands on a Title 15 (California's prison rules handbook) and study it front to back. At first, I thought she was trying to get me to learn all the rules so I could follow them, and I knew that wasn't gonna happen. But then, after a few trips to the hole, I realized that I needed to study that rule book in order to protect myself. See, not only do we as inmates have to follow rules and regulations, the K9's do, too.... And when they don't, the only way you'll be able to get them, is if you can show them that whatever they are doing wrong is written down somewhere saying it's wrong.

There was a situation at High Desert State Prison where a new Lt. was assigned to the hole and he was giving out the time for everyone who came from the yard with write-ups. Well, he was giving everyone way too much hole time and no one fought it because they were all under the assumption that since he was an Lt. they couldn't fight it. I had gotten a write-up while I was back there and in the Title 15 it says that if you catch a write-up while you're in segregation, you get less loss of privileges than if you were to have caught that same write-up on the yard. So I appealed his decision and I won. After I did it everyone else started doing it and it got to the point where other C.O.'s were talking shit behind that Lt.'s back, eventually undermining his authority by giving guys their property back before their time was up for loss of privileges. If I wouldn't have taken the time to read the fine print in the Title 15 all that fake shit would've kept going on.

Thus, it is extremely important that you learn your rights as a prisoner. There are laws written to protect us from inhumane treatment. Every prison system has their own rule book. Get your hands on yours and study it front to back. It really helps when you use their own words against them while writing grievances. Take whatever rule helps your argument and quote it exactly how it's written. Prison officials can't dispute their own rules.

Here's a few basic rights that all prisoners have:

1. ACCESS TO READING MATERIALS: Prison officials can stop you from getting or reading books that they think are dangerous or pornographic. They can also make you get all books straight from the publisher.

Even though the First Amendment protects your right to get books and magazines, it doesn't mean you can have any book you want. That right is limited by the prison's interest in maintaining order and security. On top of that, the Supreme Court has become more conservative over the last several decades which means they've given prisons a lot more power to restrict your First Amendment rights.

2. POLITICAL BELIEFS: You can believe whatever you want, yet the prison may be able to stop you from writing, talking or organizing around your beliefs.

Prison officials cannot legally punish you simply because they disagree with your beliefs. Nevertheless, they can limit your ability to express your beliefs.

3. CENSORSHIP OF MAIL: Prison guards can read your letters, and look at them to make sure there's no contraband inside. They can't really stop you from writing whatever you want to people on the outside, but they can stop certain people from writing you if they're considered dangerous.

In order to censor the letters you send to people outside prison, prison officials have to be able to prove the censorship is necessary to protect the interest of the prison. Under the Martinez rule prisons can't censor your mail just because it makes rude comments about the prison or prison staff. Prison officials can't read your legal mail, but they can open it in your presence to inspect it for contraband.

$$\$\$\$\$\$$$

$350,000 SETTLEMENT IN PLN CENSORSHIP SUIT AGAINST VENTURA COUNTY, CALIFORNIA
by Derek Gilna

In a victory for the First Amendment rights of prisoners and those who correspond with them, Prison Legal News recently obtained a substantial settlement in a lawsuit filed against the Ventura County Sheriff's Office in California.

PLN brought suit in federal district court on January 31, 2014, alleging that the sheriff's policy of limiting incoming and outgoing mail to postcards at the county jail violated PLN's right to freely distribute information, correspondence and subscription forms to prisoners at the facility.

In recent years, PLN has challenged postcard-only policies at jails across the nation with a high degree of success, arguing that such policies are unconstitutional and unreasonably restrict correspondence between prisoners and those on the outside, including their family members and children.

Ventura County attempted to justify its postcard-only policy by arguing that contraband had been sent to the jail in envelopes and prisoners were using letters to conduct criminal activity. U.S. District Court Judge George H. King found those arguments unpersuasive, and entered a preliminary injunction on May 29, 2014 that barred the sheriff's office from enforcing the postcard-only policy.

The county initially appealed the preliminary injunction order to the Ninth Circuit, but then settled the case in July 2014. Under the settlement, Ventura County agreed to a restructuring of the sheriff's policy related to prisoner mail and paid $350,000 in damages, attorney's fees and costs.

The county agreed "[to] not refuse to deliver correspondence to or from inmates at the county jails on the ground that correspondence is not written on a postcard... [to] not refuse to deliver correspondence, catalogs or subscription order forms to inmates at the jail on the basis that inmates cannot order subscriptions or other reading material... [to] not refuse to deliver correspondence to inmates at the jail that were Xeroxed, photocopies or printed from the internet... [to] not refuse to deliver copies of publications from plaintiff or other publishers on account of sexually 'suggestive' content, unless the publication contains images of exposed genitalia, buttocks or female breasts and/or graphic depictions of sexual acts, [and to] not prohibit inmates from ordering books, magazines or other publications."

The Ventura County Sheriff's Office also agreed to "conduct a four hour training block in order to adequately familiarize all mailroom staff persons with the provisions of the [new] mail policy," and "thereafter conduct two hour annual legal updates."

The district court retained jurisdiction to enforce the terms of the settlement, and entered a permanent injunction on September 4, 2014.

PLN was represented by attorneys Brian Vogel of Ventura and Ernest Galvan with the San Francisco law firm of Rosen Bien Galvan & Grunfeld, plus Lance Weber, general counsel for the Human Rights Defense Center, PLN's parent organization.

$$\$\$\$\$\$$$

4. TELEPHONE: The prison can limit the amount of calls you can make and they can monitor those calls.

The First Amendment does protect your right to talk to family and friends on the phone. However, prisons are allowed to place restrictions on phone access for prisoners confined to Special Housing Units for disciplinary reasons. And, they are allowed to limit the number of different people you can call. They can also require you to register the names on the list, subjecting them to approval from the prison.

5. VISITS: Prisons can limit your visits, but they can't permanently ban you from getting visits.
Your right to freedom of association under the First Amendment, your right to be free from cruel and unusual punishment under the Eighth Amendment,

and your right to due process under the Fifth and Fourteenth Amendment can all be argued in your favor if you're ever denied access to your visits.

6. RELIGIOUS FREEDOM: You have the right to practice your religion as long as it doesn't interfere with the security of the prison.

The First and Fourteenth Amendments as well as several federal statutes protect your freedom of religion. If your right to practice your religion is ever in jeopardy, there are five different ways you can fight for it: the Religious Land Use, Institutionalized Persons Act, the Fourteenth Amendment, the Establishment Clause, and the Free Exercise Clause.

7. FREEDOM FROM DISCRIMINATION: Prison officials can't treat you differently based on your race, religion, or gender. The prison can't segregate prisoners by race or religion except in very limit circumstances. The Fourteenth Amendment guarantees everyone "equal protection of the law." This means a prison can't treat certain prisoners better than others without a specific reason.

$$$$$

$695,000 SETTLEMENT IN DISCRIMINATION SUIT BY DEAF COLORADO DETAINEES

The City and County of Denver has paid $695,000 to settle a lawsuit that alleged systematic discrimination against deaf people detained or imprisoned at city and county jails and detention centers.

The lawsuit was filed by three former pre-trial detainees, the Colorado Cross-Disability Coalition (CCDC) and the Colorado Association for the Deaf

(CAD). The detainees were all profoundly deaf; as such, they considered American Sign Language, not English, to be their primary language. In order to communicate effectively in situations involving medical or legal advice and decision making, the detainees required the services of a qualified sign language interpreter.

Shawn Vigil was received at the Denver County Jail (DCJ) on August 28, 2005; Roger Krebs was taken into custody on March 29, 2007 and housed at the Pre-Arraignment Detention Facility (PADF); and Sarah Burke was held at a police station and the PADF after her arrest on August 29, 2007.

None of them could hear or communicate verbally due to their deafness, which was known to jail officials. Solely on the basis of their disability, they were isolated from other detainees and placed in special needs housing.

Despite that placement, the DCJ and PADG had no policy, procedure or equipment in place to accommodate the needs of deaf or hard of hearing detainees, which deprive them of effective communications with jail staff. It also prevented them from placing telephone calls to friends, family members or legal counsel.

When Vigil entered the DCJ, he faced serious charges that could have resulted in a lengthy term of incarceration. The DCJ has a policy to determine a detainee's risk of suicide; however, the inability of jail staff to communicate with Vigil rendered them unable to determine his mental status. The complaint alleged that this communication failure contributed to Vigil's suicide attempt by hanging on September 27, 2005. He died four days later after being removed from life support.

Burke had diabetes, but was unable to communicate her medical needs or her need to have something to eat because she was hyperglycemic. She was not provided with TTY device to make phone calls and was treated with callous indifference by jail staff.

On September 7, 2012, the parties reached settlement in the lawsuit. A lump sum of $695,000 was paid to the law firm of King & Greisen to cover attorney fees and damages related to Vigil's death and the emotional distress experienced by Krebs and Burke.

The settlement also provided that the federal district court would vacate its order dismissing CCDC and CAD as plaintiffs due to lack of standing. Consequently, CCDC and CAD were reinstated as plaintiffs so they could join in the settlement, which was finalized in October 2012. See: Ulibarri v. City and County of Denver, U.S.D.C. (D. Col.), Case No. 1:07-cv-01814-ODS-MJW.

$$$$$

8. DUE PROCESS RIGHTS REGARDING TRANSFERS AND SEGREGATION: You can only challenge adverse transfers or segregation if it's done to get back at you for something you have a right to do, or if it's unusually harsh.

A prison can't transfer you to punish you for complaining or to keep you from filing a lawsuit. Prison officials can't use transfers or segregation to restrict your access to the courts.

9. SEARCH AND SEIZURES: C.O.'s can search your cell whenever they want, but they're limited on when and how they can strip search you.

The Fourth Amendment forbids the government from conducting "unreasonable searches and seizures." Nevertheless, the Fourth Amendment only protects things in which you have a "reasonable expectation of privacy." The Supreme Court says prisoners don't have an expectation of privacy in their cells, but that doesn't mean all cell searches are okay.

Strip searches are generally allowed but many courts state that the searches can't be excessive or used to harass, intimidate, or punish.

$$$$$

MALE GUARD'S VIDEOTAPING OF FEMALE PRISONERS BEING STRIP SEARCHED RESULTS IN $675,000 SETTLEMENT
by David Reutter

In August 2014, a Massachusetts federal district court granted summary judgment to a class of 176 former and current prisoners who challenged a policy at the Western Regional Women's Correctional Center (WCC) that allowed male guards to videotape female prisoners being strip searched. The court held the policy violated the prisoners' Fourth Amendment rights, and the case subsequently settled.

The lawsuit was brought by lead plaintiff Debra Baggett, who spent all but nearly three weeks from September 5, 2008 to January 28, 2012 at WCC. The facility houses both pretrial detainees and sentenced prisoners from four western Massachusetts counties. The court granted class-action status in the case in May, 2011.

At issue was WCC's policy governing the transfer of prisoners into the facility's segregation unit if they presented a suicide risk, committed certain disciplinary infractions or needed to be in protective custody. The policy required a minimum of four guards to make such transfers. It also subjected each prisoner to a strip and visual body cavity search that required her to strip naked and "lift her breasts, spread her legs, bend over, and spread her buttocks." If she was menstruating, she had to remove any tampon or pad.

The objectionable portion of the WCC policy was the videotaping of such searches by male guards. From September 15, 2008 until the court's August 26, 2014 summary judgment order, male guards were present during and recorded 274 strip searches. "For 90% of these searches, two or more females were in the cell, and during 58% three or more females were present," wrote U.S. District Court Judge Michael A. Ponsor.

In what the court called a "dubious" defense, prison officials had asserted that "any videotaping by male guards occurred without the male actually looking at the female he was actually filming." The videos themselves belied that assertion, as 60% show[ed] some or all of the women's genitals, buttocks, or breasts; and 82%... show[ed] some portion of the women below the neck." The defendants' theory was "difficult to conjure up" when considering the demands of keeping the camera steady and trained on the correct location in the cell. Yet, as there was disputed material fact as to whether male guards had directly viewed the women during the searches, the court did not grant summary judgment on that issue.

It did, however, grant judgment to the plaintiffs based upon the fact that male guards were "in the immediate vicinity conducting videotaping" while the prisoners were being strip searched. The district court found it was clearly established that a prisoner's privacy rights are "violated when guards of the opposite sex regularly observe him/her engaged in personal activities such as undressing, showering, and using the toilet."

Just "the nearby presence of an individual of the opposite sex during a strip search can be in itself a deeply humiliated experience," the district court wrote. "No inmate placed in such a vulnerable and exposed position should have to rely, or comfortably would rely, on the scrupulousness of an officer of the opposite sex turning his or her head as a safeguard to the inmate's privacy and basic dignity."

Therefore, the court granted summary judgment to the class members based on the presence of male guards during the searches, held the defendants were not entitled to qualified immunity, and ordered the parties to submit plans for equitable relief and monetary damages.

The state appealed to the First Circuit. While the appeal was pending, however, the parties entered into settlement negotiations, and in March, 2015 asked the district court for preliminary approval of a settlement. Pursuant to the agreement, which was approved by the court on April 9, 2015, officials at WCC will "change their policy to prohibit male correctional officers from holding the camera during the strip searches of female inmates except in extreme circumstances." The prisoner class members will also receive a total of $675,000 including $178,000 in damages payable to the class, $475,000 in attorney fees and $22,000 in costs.

The class representative will receive $20,000 and four prisoners who had their depositions taken will each receive $2,000, payable form the damages award; other prisoner who were videotaped by male guards during strip searches will each receive approximately $875. The district court granted final approval of the class-action settlement on September 10, 2015, and the state's appeal was dismissed.

The prisoners were represented by Boston attorneys Howard Friedman and David Milton. See: Baggett v. Ashe, U.S.D.C. (D. Mass), Case No. 3:11-cv-30223-MAP.

$$$$$

10. CRUEL AND UNUASUAL PUNISHMENT: Prison officials never have the right to beat you or harm you unless they make their actions "seem" "reasonable" for the situation.

The Eighth Amendment forbids "cruel and unusual punishment." It's probably the most important amendment for prisoners. It's the source for your protection against excessive force and guard brutality.

11. YOUR RIGHT TO DECENT CONDITIONS: You do have constitutional right to humane conditions in prison. Prison officials violate the Eighth Amendment when they expose prisoners to an unreasonable risk of serious harm or deprive them of basic human needs, such as shelter, food, exercise, clothing, sanitation, and hygiene.

Below are the most common Eighth Amendment challenges to prison conditions:

- Food: Meals can't be denied as retaliation, since denying one's food can be a deprivation of a life necessity. However, prisons can serve pretty much anything they want provided it meets federal nutritional standards.

- Exercise: Prisons must provide prisoners with opportunities for exercise outside of their cells. Yet, it is generally acceptable to limit exercise opportunities for a short time or during emergencies.

- Air Quality and Temperature: Even though you are not entitled to any specific air temperature, you should be given bedding and clothing appropriate for the temperature, and not be subjected to extreme heat or cold. And, you can definitely challenge air quality when it poses a serious danger to your health.

- Sanitation and Personal Hygiene: Prisoners are entitled to basic supplies such as toothbrushes, toothpaste, soap, razors and cleaning products.

- Overcrowding: To successfully challenge overcrowding, you must show that it has caused serious deprivation of basic human needs such as food, safety, or sanitation.

$$$$$

MINNESOTA CIVIL DETAINEE RAPED BY CELLMATE RECEIVES $203,000 SETTLEMENT
by David Reutter

The state of Minnesota agreed to a $203,000 settlement in a lawsuit brought by a civil detainee at the Minnesota Sex Offender Program (MSOP) that alleged a policy or custom of disregarding patient safety resulting in the detainee suffering "a brutal physical and sexual assault by his roommate."

MSOP detainee Michael Mrozek, 24, was celled with Brian Sorenson, 38, who allegedly had a "history of violent and harassing actions toward other patients" as well as a "history of sexually predatory conduct" that had resulted in his commitment to MSOP.

The complaint alleged that "on or about December 18, 2010" Sorenson sat down on Mrozek's bed as he was trying to go to sleep. His close proximity made Mrozek uncomfortable. In response to Mrozek's request for Sorenson to leave, Sorenson instead laid down on the bed next to him.

Sorenson then went back to his own bed, but began discussing how they could "sexually act out without getting caught." Sorenson then asked Mrozek "what he would do if he woke up in the middle of the night and found someone standing over him."

Both Mrozek and Sorenson reported the incident to their separate "core groups" a group of detainees who live in the same unit and meet in therapy sessions facilitated by MSOP staffers. The members in Sorenson's group insisted that he be moved to another cell to protect Mrozek's safety, but MSOP staff took no action other than documenting the incident.

Shortly after midnight on December 30, 2010, Sorenson began physically assaulting Mrozek, slapping him and threatening further harm. Sorenson demanded that Mrozek perform oral sex or consent to anal sex. In the face of Mrozek's refusals, Sorenson forcibly removed Mrozek's clothing, made him perform oral sex and forcibly sodomized him. He continued to hit Mrozek and placed a belt around his neck while threatening to kill him. MSOP records showed that at about 1:50 a.m., Mrozek was finally able to activate the cell's intercom to alert staff about the assault.

Sorenson subsequently admitted to attacking Mrozek, pleaded guilty to first-degree criminal sexual conduct and was transferred to a state prison. Mrozek filed suit against MSOP officials in federal court, and the case settled after three years of litigation.

The settlement provides that Mrozek receive $131,102.90 in damages and his counsel, Jordan Jusher, receive $71,897.10 in attorney fees and costs. The state also paid the cost of the mediation hearing and waived a $1,072.04 medical assistance tort recovery claim for Morzek's medical treatment. Finally, Minnesota Department of Human Services Deputy Commissioner Anne M. Barry issued a letter of apology to to Mrozek, stating the agency "sincerly regrets the sexual assault" that he endured. See: Mrozek v. Ringler, U.S.D.C. (D. Mnn.), Case No. 0:11-cv-02572-JRT-SER.

$$$$$

12. YOUR RIGHT TO MEDICAL CARE: The Eighth Amendment doesn't protect you from medical malpractice, but it does ensure that you're provided with medical care while incarcerated.

If you feel like your right to medical care has been violated, the Constitution isn't the only source of your legal rights. You can also bring a medical malpractice suit in state court.

Also, the Constitution protects your right to have your sensitive medical information private, this means you can sue somebody if someone runs their mouth about your health or status.

$$$$$

GEORGIA: $453,000 JURY VERDICT AGAINST PRIVATE JAIL MEDICAL CONTRACTOR
by David Reutter

A Georgia federal jury awarded $452.917.00 to a former detainee for injuries that resulted from inadequate medical care at the Hart County Jail.

Monica Robinson was on probation for a criminal offense on April 20, 2012 when she went to a hospital emergency room for treatment of a rash that had recently appeared. Four days later she returned to the emergency room because the rash had progressed.

She spent the next five days in the hospital after testing indicated she had a MRSA infection. She also tested positive for amphetamines. Following her release from the hospital. Robinson received antibiotics to take orally She was arrested on July 21, for failing to comply with the terms of her probation; upon booking, she said she was in pain and had been recently hospitalized for a staph infection.

The next morning Robinson requested medical attention for her pain complaints. Without seeing a medical professional, she was given Motrin and Benadryl. Between July 23, and August 11, 2012, she continued to complain that she had a staph infection, her shoulder and back hurt, and she was constipated.

The only medical attention provided was from an EMT who prescribed pain medication. EMT Brian Evans noted that Robinson had a distended abdomen, yet did nothing but prescribe stool softener and Motrin.

Shortly afterwards, Robinson required physical assistance to get to the jail's medical station. She complained to EMT Mike Adams of numbness in the legs and inability to walk or urinate. He did nothing other than note the jail should "consider" sending her to a doctor if her condition did not improve.

The next morning Robinson urinated on herself. Two ministers visiting the jail saw her condition and called her family. They called Capt. Milford. He contacted Chief Deputy Tommy Whitmire to advise that Robinson was on the floor and could not get up. Whitmire ordered the jail's medical contractor, Bruce Bailer, an EMT who owns Integrated Detention Health Service (IDHS), to be called. Bailer said, "he would see what he could do." Witmire, apparently not satisfied, ordered an ambulance.

Robinson underwent surgery to treat discitis, osteomyelitis and a large epidural abscess with spinal cord compression caused by a caterial infection. While the surgery reversed the partial paralysis, Robinson still suffered a significant impairment. Prior to leaving the jail and before surgery, jail officials tried to have Robinson released from custody, and subsequently convinced the probation officer to drop charges to avoid the medical costs to treat her.

IDHS holds the contract to provide health care to detainees at the Hart County Jail. The physician of record, Dr. Robert J. Williams, was required by policy to make weekly visits to the facility. In a summary judgment order, the district court said, "Dr. Williams has never visited the jail in the years he has served as medical director, nor has he monitored the paramedics in person." Bailer had not been to the jail in three or four years, leaving EMT's Adams and Evans as the only on-site medical personnel while Robinson was incarcerated.

Robinson's suit alleged state law negligence claims and Eighth and Fourteenth Amendment violations. On August 16, 2014, a federal jury found Dr. Williams 33% liable and IDHS 67% liable for $300,000 in general damages and $152,917.50 in medical bills. Robinson was represented by attorneys Craig T. Jones and Douglas C. Mckillip. See: Robinson v. Integrated Detention Health Services, U.S.D.C. (M.D. Georgia), Case No. 3:12-cv-00020--CAR.

$$$$$

13. YOUR RIGHT TO THE COURTS: Prisoners have a right to access the courts. This right is based on the First, Fifth and Fourteenth Amendments to the Constitution.

The Supreme Court has established that prisoners have fundamental right to access the courts. This right allows you to file a Section 1983 or Bivens claim habeas petitions, or work on your criminal case. This right is so fundamental that it requires a prison to find a way for you to have meaningful access to the court.

However, even if your prison isn't allowing you to use the law library and isn't giving you legal help, you still can't necessarily win a lawsuit about it. To win, courts will require you to show that you had a legitimate claim that you lost or were unable to bring, due to an action by prison officials, or inadequacy of your access to legal assistance.

CHAPTER 9

CONCLUSION

"The apparent individual conflict of the patient is revealed as a universal conflict of his environment and epoch. Neurosis is thus nothing less than an individual attempt, however unsuccessful, to solve a universal problem."--C.G. Jung.

Throughout this book I have purposely kept the vibe light. That's my style of teaching. I try to make things as simple as possible. And, it really is. This lawsuit thing really isn't that hard. All you gotta do is exhaust all local remedies (grievances), then send some motions to the courts. The rest will be done for you, and if your case has merit the judge will give you a lawyer for free. Don't let no one tell you its hard, cuz it's not.

Now that we're at the end of this journey, I wanna get serious. I want to get deeper into the underlying problem which is that we're actually in prison in the first place. The degree at which our people are being locked up is as important to our physical and mental health as our poverty, drop-out and fatality rates. Our incarceration isn't just an act against individuals. The assault is against all Americans. The closer you look, the more it will be obvious that there are intense structures at work against us.

We must always keep in mind that there is a countrywide offensive against the middle and lower classes. And that we're under attack every minute of every day, with whatever weapons the government can come up with. The truth of the matter is that this assault hasn't let up since Yacub first laid his greedy hands on power many centuries ago.

Our confinement and isolation has always been an essential part of this process of our systematic destruction. Those they don't kill, they control through fear of imprisonment. Imprisonment remains one of their most effective methods for physically, emotionally and spiritually tearing men and women away from their families and loved ones.

Our society is destroying people. This truth is only meaningful if we know that it destroys poor Americans significantly more than the rich. Therefore, as principled social scientists, we must operate out of an intellectual framework that argues that the total population is the rod by which things should be measured. In the view of racial statistics, a certain racial group's percent of the general population should be the same as, or at least similar to their proportions in all things good and bad in that populous. If they are 15% of the population, then they should be about 15% of all law enforcement, 15% of all prisoners, 15% of all doctors and so on...

Thus operating on this assumption, there shouldn't be one specific race or social class who disproportionately dominates this society's negative social indicators. Since black and brown people represent around 23% of this nation's population, we should account for somewhere near 23% of this nation's prison population, not well over 87%.

Unless you believe that minorities are genetically criminal, that we're born murderers, dope fiends and rapists, as the people who have manufactured this image of us have tried to brainwash us into believing then you can plainly see for yourself that there's something dangerously wrong here. Through scientific understanding we know that criminal behavior is a direct function of the people in which the individual is a product of; the society in which that individual or group is associated with. It is a people's cultural essence which regulates the presence and normality of criminal behavior. Individuals simply operate within the ranges allowed within this framework. Their morals are shaped by the dominance of calm and peace or rage and hostility at the cultural level. So we can safely say that crime is socially created and regulated. Individuals make choices within cultural and social factors.

With this information readily at our fingertips we should be able to see past the watered down versions of our own government. They have been cloaking themselves in a false image of righteousness. The criminal chaos we see all around us today isn't the function of a few hardheads. It's a normal social personality, bred within a deranged cultural framework.

A criminal culture automatically creates even greater levels of destruction among those most oppressed, as they seek release from their want and frustrations by projecting their powerlessness on the only ones they are unafraid to attack: each other. And that's when they themselves get captured and incarcerated in the criminal justice system.

With that in mind, let's take a few moments to look at the numbers of us who are being held captive within the belly of this horrendous beast. This is the only way we can truly see the injustices and come face to face with the creators of our collective destruction.

Statistics about this prison system speak for themselves. First of all, even though the people in this country constitute only about 11% of the world's population, the prisoners of this country make up 26% of all persons behind bars on the planet. This country has the highest incarceration rate in the world. There are well over two million people behind bars in this country. The federal government has estimated that 18.2% of all black and brown men between the ages of 25 and 29 are in jails and prisons, compared with only 1.9% of white men in that age group.

To kill people on a spiritual level, you must keep them from being whole.

You must remove the possibility of them being a family. Where you cannot make the men and women hate and blame each other for the tragedy forced on them by others, you must remove the possibility of them touching each other in love. You must physically separate their children from them, with the end goal of driving them emotionally and physically away from them. You must build insurmountable mental and physical walls between them. Then their children are yours to do with as you please. And that's when they will finally begin to confuse their enemies' lies and aggressions with love.

The harvesting of our men has been going on for so long that now we have begun to seriously take notice of a longstanding trend toward what is being called intergenerational incarceration. Sons, their fathers and grandfathers are finding themselves all locked up in the same prison facility. There is every reason to believe that this tragic family reunion has already begun to include the fourth and fifth generations.

What may be equally appalling is that those responsible for arresting and knowingly prosecuting innocent men are left untouched by the criminal justice system, even after they are revealed for the maliciously deceitful criminals that they are. With respect to the few cases where falsely convicted individuals are given a court ordered monetary compensation for their loss, the community is still victimized. We continue to finance our own destruction. When we get so excited over these victories, we forget that the money used to pay these compensations are coming out of our own pockets. When we jump around celebrating some individual winning this or that very minor monetary award, we forget that the money for the awards almost excursively comes from our local tax dollars. They don't come out of the pay of those who committed the acts. They come out of the tax dollars of the residence who live in the community of those whom the acts were committed against. We're the ones who live in and provide the majority of the tax base in those areas in which we are violated. Therefore, the millions and millions of dollars paid out in justified lawsuits for violations others commit are paid by us.

We are paying the penalty for being violated. We are being charged for the damages of those who legally abuse us out of our own pockets. The individuals who commit these crimes against us don't live in our community; they don't pay taxes in our communities. Therefore, they don't suffer for their crimes. They commit these crimes against us and are rewarded for doing it. Crime truly does pay! When falsely convicted men and women are paid money by the court for their losses, it in no way negatively impacts the individuals who committed these acts of brutality.

A family rewards its member when they do well, when they serve and protect them from others they perceive as threats to their safety. So these criminal judges and prosecutors are applauded by their community with employment income for their efforts to beat, torture and otherwise keep us at bay. They continue to be honored as hardworking, dedicated agents of this racist government.

We must continue to remember that prison is only one aspect of a genocidal effort. It is only one instrument which is connected in so many other pieces in the war against us.

Positive Energy Always Creates Elevation. That's Peace!
King Guru

DISTRICT COURTS

We've already discussed the fact that the Federal Judiciary system is broken down into districts. Some states have more than one district and some districts have more than one division. First, you find out what county your prison is located in and then you can figure out what district to file your lawsuit in. Here's a list of all the district courts in the country:

ALABAMA (11th Circuit)

Northern District of
Alabama: Bibb, Blunt,
Calhoun Cherokee, Clay,
Clebourne,
Colbert, Cullman, Dekalb,
Etowah, Fayette, Franklin,
Greene, Jackson, Lamar,
Lauderdale, Lawrence,
Limestone, Madison,
Marion, Marshall, Morgan,
Pickens, Randolph, Saint
Clair, Shelby, Sumter,
Talladega, Tuscaloosa,
Walker, Winston

United States District Court
Hugo L. Black
U.S. Courthouse

1729 Fifth Avenue North
Birmingham, AL 35203

MIDDLE DISTRICT OF ALABAMA

The Northern Division:
Autauga, Barbour, Bullock,
Butler, Chilton, Coosa,
Covington, Crenshaw,
Elmore, Lowndes,
Montgomery, and Pike.

The Southern Division:
Coffee, Dale, Geneva,
Henry, Houston

The Eastern Division:
Chambers, Lee, Macon,
Randolph, Russell,
Tallapoosa

Ms. Debra Hackett Clerk of
Court
One Church Street
Montgomery, AL 36104

Southern District of
Alabama: Baldwin, Choctaw,
Clarke, Conceuh, Dallas,
Escambia, Hale, Marengo,
Mobile, Monroe, Perry,
Washington, Wilcox

U.S. Courthouse
143 St. Joseph Street
Mobile, AL 36602

ALASKA (9th Circuit)

District of Alaska
U.S. District Court Clerk's
Office
222 W. 7th Avenue, #4
Anchorage, AK 99513

ARIZONA (9th Circuit)

District of Arizona
Pheonix Division: Maricopa,
Pinal, Yuma, La Paz, Gila
Prescott Division: Apache,
Navajo, Coconino, Mohave,
Yavapi

97

Sandra Day O'Connor U.S. Courthouse
401 West Washington Street, Suite 130, SPC 1
Phoenix, AZ 85003

Tucson Division: Pima, Cochise, Santa Cruz, Graham, Greenlee, Evo A. DeConcim

U.S. Courthouse
405 West Congress Street, Suite 1500
Tucson, AZ 85701

ARKANSAS (8th Circuit)

Eastern District of Arkansas Northern Division 1:
Cleburne, Fulton, Independence Izard, Jackson, Sharp, Stone

Eastern division 2: Cross, Lee, Monroe, Phillips, St. Francis and Woodruff

Western Division 4:
Conway, Fulkner, Lonoke, Perry, Pope, Prairie, Pulaski, Saline, Van Buren, White, Yell

Pine Bluff Division 5:
Arkansas, Chicot, Cleveland, Dallas, Desha, Drew, Grant, Jefferson and Lincoln

U.S. District Court Clerk's Office

U.S. Post Office & Courthouse
600 West Capitol, #402
Little Rock, AR 72201-3325

Jonesboro Division 3: Clay, Craighead, Crittenden, Greene, Lawrence, Missippi Poinsett, Randolph

U.S. District Court Clerk's Office
P.O. Box 7080
Jonesboro, AR 72403

WESTERN DISTRICT OF ARKANSAS

El Dorado Division 1:
Ashley, Bradley, Calhoun, Columbia, Ouachita, Union

U.S. District Court Clerk's Office
205 United States Courthouse & Post Office
P.O. Box 1566
El Dorado, AR 71730-1566

Fort Smith Division 2:
Crawford, Franklin, Johnson, Logan, Polk, Scott, Sebastian U.S.

District Court Clerk's Office
1038 Isaac C. Parker Federal Building
P.O. Box 1547
Fort Smith, AR 72902-1547

Harrison Division 3: Baxter, Boone, Carroll, Marion, Newton and Searcy

U.S. District Court Clerk's Office
523 Federal Building
35 East Mountain Street
P.O. Box 6420
Fayetteville, AR 72702-6420

Texarkana Division 4: Hempstead, Howard, Lafayette, Little River, Miller, Nevada and Sevier

U.S. District Court Clerk's Office
302 U.S. Post Office and Courthouse
500 State Line Blvd.
P.O. Box 2746
Texarkana, AR 75504-2746

Fayetteville Division 5: Benton, Madison, Washington

U.S. District Court Clerk's Office
523 Federal Building
35 East Mountain Street
P.O. Box 6420
Fayetteville, AR 72702-6420

Hot Springs Division 6: Clark, Garland, Hot Spring, Montgomery, Pike

U.S. District Court Clerk's Office

347 U.S. Post Office and Courthouse
Reserve and Broadway Streets P.O. Drawer 1 Hot Springs, AR 72902-4143

CALIFORNIA (9th Circuit)

Northern District of California: Alameda, Contra Costa, Del Norte, Humboldt, Lake, Mann, Mendocino, Monterey, Napa, San Benito, San Francisco, San Mateo, Santa Clara, Santa Cruz, Sonoma

U.S. District Courthouse Clerk's Office
450 Golden Gate Ave., 16th floor San Francisco, CA 94102
Eastern Division of California

Fresno Division: Calaveras, Fresno, Inyo, Kern, Kings, Madera, Mariposa, Merced, Stanislaus, Tulare and Tuolumne

U.S. District Court
1130 0 Street
Fresno, CA 93721

Sacramento Division: Alpine, Amador, Butte, Colusa, El Dorado, Glenn, Lassen, Modoc, Mono, Nevada, Placer, Plumas, Sacramento, San Joaquin,

Shasta Sierra, Siskiyou,
Solano, Sutter, Tehama,
Trinity, Yolo, Yuba

U.S. District Court
501 I Street, Suite 4-401
Sacramento, CA 95814

Central District of California:
Los Angeles, Orange
County, Riverside, San
Bernardino, San Luis
Obispo, Santa Barbara,
Ventura

U.S. Courthouse
312 N. Spring Street
Los Angeles, CA 90012

Southern District of
California:
Imperial, San Diego
Office of the Clerk U.S.
District Court
Southern District of
California
880 Front Street, Suite 4290
San Diego, CA 92101-8900

COLORADO (10th Circuit)

District of Colorado
Clerk's Office
Alfred A. Arraj United States
Courthouse
Room A-105 901 19th Street
Denver, Colorado 80294-
3589

CONNECTICUT (2d Circuit)

District of Connecticut
U.S. Courthouse
141 Church Street
New Haven, CT

DELAWARE (3d Circuit)

District of Delaware
U.S. District Court
844 N. King Street Lockbox
18
Wilmington, DE 19801

DISTRICT OF COLUMBIA (D.C. Circuit)

District for the District of
Columbia
United States District Court
for the District of Columbia
333 Constitution Avenue,
N.W.
Washington, D.C. 20001

FLORIDA

Northern District of Florida
Pensacola Division:
Escambia, Santa Rosa,
Okaloosa, Walton

U.S. Federal Courthouse
1 North Palafox St.
Pensacola, FL 32502

Panama City Division:
Jackson, Holmes,
Washington, Bay Calhoun,
Gulf

U.S. Federal Courthouse

30 W. Government St.
Panama City, FL 32401

Tallahassee Division: Leon,
Gadsden, Liberty Franklin,
Wakulla, Jefferson, Taylor,
Madison

U.S. Federal Courthouse
111 N. Adams Street
Tallahassee, FL 32301

Gainesville division:
Alachua, Lafayette, Dixie,
Gilchrist, Levy

U.S. Federal Courthouse
401 S.E. First Ave. Rm. 243
Gainesville, FL 32601

MIDDLE DISTRICT OF FLORIDA

Tampa Division: Hardee,
Hernando, Hillsborough,
Manatee, Pasco, Pinellas,
Polk, Sarasota Clerk's Office,
United States District Court
Sam M Gibbons

U.S. Courthouse
801 N. Florida Avenue, Rm.
218
Tampa, Florida 33602-3800

Ft. Myers Division:
Charlotte, Collier, DeSoto,
Glades, Hendry, Lee Clerk's
Office,

United States District Court
U.S. Courthouse & Federal
Building
2110 First Street, Rm. 2-194
Fort Myers, FL 33901-3083

Orlando Division: Brevard,
Orange, Osceola, Seminole,
Volusia

Clerk's Office, United States
District Court George C.
Young U.S. Courthouse
80 N. Hughey Avenue, Rm.
300
Orlando, FL 32801-9975

Jacksonville Division: Baker,
Bradford, Clay, Columbia,
Duval,Flagler, Hamilton,
Nassau, Putnam, St. Johns,
Suwanne, Union

Clerk's Office, United States
District Court
Golden-Collum Memorial
Federal Building and U.S.
Courthouse
207 N.W. Second Street,
Rm. 337
Ocala, FL 34475-6666

Southern District of Florida:
Broward, Collier, Dade,
Glades, Hendry, Highlands,
Indian River, Martin,
Monroe, Okeechobee, Palm
Beach, St. Lucie

United States District Court
Clerk's Office

101

299 East Broward Boulevard
Room 108
Fort Lauderdale, FL 34950

GEORGIA (11th Circuit)

Northern District of Georgia:
Banks, Barrow, Bartow,
Carroll, Catoosa, Chattooga,
Cherokee, Calyton, Cobb,
Coweta, Dade, Dawson,
DeKalb, Douglas, Fannin,
Fayette, Floyd, Forsyth,
Fulton, Gilmer, Gordon,
Gwinnett, Habersham, Hall.,
Haralson, Heard, Henry,
Jackson, Lumpkin,
Meriwether, Murray,
Newton, Paulding, Pickens,
Pickens, Pike, Polk, Rabun,
Rockdale, Spalding,
Stephens, Towns, Troup,
Union, Walker, White,
Whitfield

U.S. Federal Courthouse
111 N. Adams Street
Tallahassee, FL 32301

MIDDLE DISTRICT OF GEORGIA

Albany Division: Baker,
Ben, Hill, Calhoun, Crisp,
Dougherty, Early, Lee,
Miller, Mitchell, Schley,
Sumter, Terrell, Turner,
Worth, Webster

U.S. District Court Clerk's
Office
P.O. Box 1906

Albany, GA 31702

Athens Division: Clarke,
Elbert, Franklin, Greene,
Hart, Madison, Morgan,
Oconee, Oconee, Oglethorpe,
Walton

U.S. District Court Clerk's
Office
P.O. Box 1106
Athens, GA 30603

Columbus Division:
Chattahoochee, Clay, Harris,
Marion, Muscogee, Quitman,
Randolph, Stewart, Talbot,
Taylor

U.S. District Court Clerk's
Office
P.O. Box 124
Columbus, GA 31902

Macon Division: Baldwin,
Bibb, Bleckley, Butts,
Crawford, Dooly, Hancock,
Houston, Jasper, Jones,
Lamar, Macon, Monroe,
Peach, Putnam, Twiggs,
Upson, Washington, Wilcox,
Wilkinson

U.S. District Court Clerk's
Office
P.O. Box 128
Macon, GA 31202

Thomasville Division:
Brooks, Colquitt, Decatur,
Grady, Seminole, Thomas
Valdosta Division: Berrien,

Clinch, Cook, Echols, Irwin,
Lanier, Lowndes, Tift

U.S. District Court Clerk's
Office
P.O. Box 68
Valdosta, GA 31601

Southern District of Georgia
Augusta Division: Burke,
Columbia, Glascock,
Jefferson, Lincoln,
McDuffie, Richmond,
Tauaferro, Warren, Wilkes

Dublin Division: Dodge,
Johnson, Lanrens,
Montgomery, Telfair,
Treutlen, Wheeler

Clerk's Office, U.S.
Courthouse
500 East Ford Street
Augusta, GA 30901

Savannah Division: Bryan,
Chatham, Effingham, Liberty

Waycross Division:
Atkinson, Bacon, Brantley,
Charlton, Coffee, Pierce,
Warc

Statesboro Division: Bulloch,
Candler, Emanuel, Evans,
Jenkins, Screven, Toombs,
Tatnall

Clerk's Office, U.S.
Courthouse
125 Bull Street, Room 304
Savannah, GA 31401

Brunswick Division:
Appling, Glynn, Jeff Davis,
Long, McIntosh, Wayne

Clerk's Office, U.S.
Courthouse
801 Gloucester Street, Suite
220
Brunswick, GA 31520

GUAM (9th Circuit)

District of Guam
U.S. Courthouse, 4th floor
520 West Soledad Avenue
Hagatna, Guam 96910

HAWAII (9th Circuit)

District of Hawaii
U.S. Courthouse
300 Ala Moana Blvd., Room
C338
Honolulu, HI 96813

IDAHO (9th Circuit)

District of Idaho
Southern Division: Ada,
Adams, Boise, Canyon,
Elmore, Gem, Owyhee,
Payette, Valley, Washington

James A. McClure Federal
Building and United States
Courthouse
550 W. Fort St.
Boise, ID 83724

Northern Division: Benewah, Bonner, Boundary, Kootenai, Shoshone

U.S. Courthouse
205 N 4th St - Rm 202
Coeur d'Alene, ID 83814

Central Division: Clearwater, Idaho, Latah, Lewis, Nez, Perce

U.S. Courthouse
220 E 5th St - Rm 304
Moscow, ID 83843

Eastern Division: Bannock, Bear Lake, Bingham, Blaine, Bonneville, Butte, Camas, Caribou, Cassia, Clark, Custer, Franklin, Fremont, Gooding, Jefferson, Jerome, Lincoln, Lemhi, Madison, Minidoka, Oneida, Power, Teton, Twin Falls

U.S. Courthouse
801 E. Sherman St.
Pocatello, ID 83201

ILLINOIS (7th Circuit)

Northern District of Illinois
Western Division: Boone, Carroll, DeKaib, Jo Davies, Lee, McHenry, Ogle, Stephenson, Whiteside, Winnebago

United States Courthouse
211 South Court Street
Rockford, Illinois 61101

Eastern Division: Cook, Dupage, Grundy, Kane, Kendall, Lake, LaSalle, Will
Everett McKinley Dirksen
Building 219 South Dearborn Street
Chicago, Illinois 60604

Central District of Illinois
Peoria Division: Bureau, Fulton, Hancock, Knox, Livingston, Marshall, McDonough, McLean, Pedria, Putnam, Stark, Tazewell, Woodford

309 U.S. Courthouse
100 N.E. Monroe Street
Peoria, IL 61602

Rock Island Division: Henderson, Henry, Mercer, Rock Island, Warren

40 U.S. Courthouse 211 19th Street
Rock Island, IL 61201

Springfield Division: Adams, Brown, Cass, Christian, DeWitt, Greene, Logan, Macoupin, Mason, Menard, Montgomery, Pike Calhoun, Sangamon, Schuyler, Scott, Shelby

151 U.S. Courthouse 600 E. Monroe Street Springfield, IL 62701

Urbana Division:
Champaign, Coles, Douglas,
Edgar, Ford, Iroquois,
Kankakee, Macon,

Moultrie, Piatt
218 U.S. Courthouse 201 S.
Vine Street
Urbana, IL 61802

Southern District of Illinois:
Alexander, Bond, Calhoun,
Clark, Clay, Clinton,
Crawford, Cumberland,
Edwards, Effingham,
Fayette, Franklin, Gallatin,
Hamilton, Hardin, Jackson,
Jasper, Jefferson, Jersey,
Johnson, Lawrence,
Madison, Marrion, Marshall,
Massac, Monroe, Perry,
Pope, Pulaski, Randolph,
Richland, St. Clair, Saline,
Union, Wabash, Washington,
Wayne, White, Williamson

U.S. Courthouse
301 West Main Street
Benton, IL 62812

INDIANA (7th Circuit)

Northern District of Indiana
Fort Wayne Division:
Adams, Allen, Blackford,
DeKalb, Grant, Huntington,
Jay, LaGrange, Noble
Steuben, Wells, Whitley

U.S. Courthouse
1300 S. Harrison St.
Fort Wayne, IN 46802

Hammond Division: Lake,
Porter

U.S. Courthouse
5400 Federal Plaza
Hammond, IN 46320

Lafayette Division: Benton,
Carroll, Jasper, Newton,
Tippecanoe, Warren, White

U.S. Courthouse
230 N. Fourth St.
Lafayette, IN 47901

South Bend Division: Cass,
Elkhart, Fulton, Kosciusko,
LaPorte, Marshall, Miami,
Pulaski, St. Joseph, Starke,
Wabash

U.S. Courthouse
204 S. Main St.
South Bend, IN 46601

Southern District of Indiana
Indianapolis Division:
Bartholomew, Boone,
Brown, Clinton, Decatur,
Delaware, Fayette, Fountain,
Franklin, Hamilton,
Hancock, Hendricks, Henry,
Howard, Johnson, Madison,
Marion, Monroe,
Montgomery, Morgan,
Randolph, Rush, Shelby,
Tipton, Union, Wayne
Birch Bay

Federal Building and United States Courthouse 46 East Ohio Street, Room 105 Indianapolis, IN 46204

Terre Haute Division: Caly, Greene, Knox, Owen, Parke, Putnam, Sullivan, Vermillion, Vigo
207 Federal Building
30 North Seventh Street
Terre
Haute, IN 47808

Evansville Division: Daviess, Dubois, Gibson, Martin, Perry, Pike, Posey, Spencer,

Vanderburgh, Warrick
304 Federal Building
101 Northwest MLK
Boulevard
Evansville, IN 47708

New Albany Division: Cairk, Crawford, Dearborn, Floyd, Harrison, Jackson, Jefferson, Jennings, Lawrence, Ohio, Orage, Ripley, Scott,

Switzerland, Washington
210 Federal Building 121
West Spring Street New
Albany, IN 47150

IOWA (8th Circuit)

Northern District of Iowa
Cedar Rapids Division:
Benton, Cedar, Grundy,
Hardin, Iowa, Jones, Linn,
Tama

Eastern Division: Allamakee, Blackhawk, Bremer, Buchanan, Chickasaw, Clayton, Delaware, Dubuque, Fayette, Floyd, Howard, Jackson, Mitchell, Winneshiek

U.S. District Court for the
Northern District of Iowa
P.O. Box 74710
Cedar Rapids, IA 52407-
4710

Western Division: Buena Vista, Cherokee, Clay, Crawford, Dickinson, Ida, Lyon, Monona, O'Brien, Osceola, Plymouth, Sac, Sioux, Woodbury

Central Division: Butler, Calhoun, Carroll, Cerro, Gordo, Emmet, Franklin, Hamilton, Hancock, Humboldt, Kossuth, Palo Alto, Pocahontas, Webster, Winnebago, Worth, Wright

U.S. District Court for the
Northern District of Iowa
320 Sixth Street
Sioux City, IA 51101

Southern District of Iowa
Central Division: Adaire, Adams, Appanoose, Boone, Clarke, Dallas, Davis, Decatur, Greene, Guthri, Jasper, Jefferson, Keokuk, Lucas, Madison, Mahaska, Marion, Marshall, Monroe,

P1k, Poweshiek, Ringgold,
Story, Taylor, Union,
Wapello, Warren, Wayne

U.S. Courthouse
123 E. Walnut St., Room 300
P.O. Box 9344
Des Moines, IA 50306-9344

Western Division: Audubon,
Cass, Freemont, Harrison,
Mills, Montgomery, Page,
Pottawattamie, Shelby

Clerk, U.S. District Court 6th
& Broadway, Room 313 P.O.
Box 307
Council Bluffs, IA 51502

Davenport Division: Clinton,
Des Moines, Henry, Johnson,
Lee, Louisa, Muscatine,
Scott, Van Buren,
Washington

Clerk, U.S. District Court
211 19th Street
Rock Island, IL 61201

KANSAS (10th Circuit)

District of Kansas
500 State Ave 259 U.S.
Courthouse
Kansas City, Kansas 66101

KENTUCKY (6th Circuit)

Eastern District of Kentucky:
Anderson, Bath, Bell, Boone,
Bourbon, Boyd, Boyle,
Bracken, Breathitt,

Campbell, Carroll, Carter,
Clark, Clay, Elliott, Estill,
Fayette, Fleming, Floyd,
Granklin, Gallatin, Garrard,
Grant, Greenup, Harlan,
Harrison, Henry, Jackson,
Jessamine, Johnson, Kenton,
Knott, Knox, Laurel,
Lawrence, Lee, Leslie,
Lercher, Lewis, Lincoln,
McCreary, Madison
Magoffin, Martin, Mason,
Menifee, Mercer,
Montgomery, Morgan,
Nicholas, own, Owsley,
Pendleton, Perry, Pike,
Powell, Pulaski, Robertson,
Rockcastle, Rowan, Scott,
Shelby, Trimble, Wayne,
Whitley, Wolfe, Woodford

Leslie G. Whitmer, Clerk
101 Barr St. Room 206 P.O
Drawer 3074
Lexington, KY 40588

Western District of Kentucky
Bowling Green Division:
Adair, Allen, Barren, Butler,
Casey, Clinton, Cumberland,
Edmonson, Green, Hart,
Logan, Metcalf, Monroe,
Russell, Simpson, Taylor,
Todd,

Warren Clerks Office
241 East Main Street, Suite
120 Bowling Green, KY
42101-2175

Louisville Division:
Breckinridge, Bullitt, Hardin,

107

Jefferson, Larue, Marion, Meade, Nelson, Oldham, Spencer,

Washington Clerks Office
601 W. Broadway, Room 106 Gene Snyder Courthouse
Louisville, KY 40202

Owensboro Division: Daviess, Grayson, Hancock, Henderson, Hopkins, McLean, Muhlenberg, Ohio, Union,

Webster Clerks Office
423 Frederica Street, suite 126
Owensboro, KY 42301-3013

Paducah Division: Ballard, Caldwell, Calloway, Carlisle, Christian, Crittenden, Fulton, Graves, Hickman, Limington, Lyon, McCracken, Marshall, Trigg

Clerk's Office
501 Broadway, Suite 127
Paducah, KY 42001-6801

LOUISIANA (5th Circuit)

Eastern District of Louisiana: Assumption, Jefferson, Lafourche, Orleans, Plaquemines, Saint Bernard, Saint Charles, Saint James, Saint John the Baptist, Saint Tammany, Tangipaho Terrebonne, Washington

U.S. District Court
500 Camp Street, Room C-151
New Orleans, LA 70130

Middle District of Louisiana: Ascension, East Baton Rouge, East Feliciana, Iberville, Livingston, Pointe Coupee, Saint Helena, West Baton Rouge, West Feliciana

U.S. District Court
777 Florida Street, Suite 139
Baton Rouge, LA 70801

Western District of Louisiana: Acadia, Allen, Avoyelles, Beauregard, Bienville, Bossier, Caddo, Calacasieu, Caldwell, Cameron, Catahoula, Caliborne, Concordia, Jefferson Davis, De Soto, East Carroll, Evangeline, Frnaklin, Grant, Iberia, Jackson, Lafayette, La Salle, Lincoln, Madison, Morehouse, Natchitoches, Ouachita, Rapides, Red River, Richland, Sabine, Saint Landry, Saint Martin, Saint Mary, Tensas, Union, Vermilion, Vernon, Webster, West Carroll, Winn

Robert H. Shemwell, Clerk
300 Fannin St., Ste. 1167
Shreveport, LA 71101-3083

MAINE (1st Circuit)

District of Maine
Bangor Division:
Arronstrook, Franklin,
Hancock, Kennebec,
Penobscot, Piscataquis,
Somerset, Waldo,
Washington

Clerk, U.S. District Court
202 Harlow Street, Room
357
P.O. Box 1007
Bangor, Maine 04330

Portland Division:
Androscoggin, Cumberland,
Knox, Lincoln, Oxford,
Sagadahoc,

York Clerk, U.S. District
Court
156 Federal Street
Portland, Maine 04101

MARYLAND (4th Circuit)

District of Maryland
U.S. Courthouse
101 W. Lombard Street
Baltimore, MD 21201

MASSACHUSETTS (9th Circuit)

District of Massachusetts
Eastern Division: Barnstable,
Bristol, Dukes, Essex,
Middlesex, Nantucket,
Norfolk, Plymouth, Suffolk

John Joseph Moakley
United States Courthouse

1 Courthouse Way - Suite
2300
Boston, MA 02210

Central Division: Worcester
County

Harold D. Donohue Federal
Building & Courthouse
595 Main Street - Rm 502
Worcester, MA 01608

Western Division: Berkshire,
Franklin, Hampden,
Hampshire

Federal Building &
Courthouse
1550 Main Street
Springfield, MA 01103

MICHIGAN (6th Circuit)

Eastern District of Michigan:
Alcona, Alpena, Arenac,
Bay, Cheboygan, Clare,
Crawford, Genesee,
Gladwin, Gratiot, Huron,
Iosco, Isabella, Jackson,
Lapeer, Lenawee,
Libingston, Macomb,
Midland, Monroe,
Montmorency, Oakland,
Ogemaw, Oscodo, Otsego,
Presque Isle, Roscommon,
Saginaw, Saint Clair,
Sanilac, Shiawassee,
Tuscola, Washtenaw, Wayne

U.S. District Courthouse
200 E. Liberty Street Ann
Arbor, MI 48104

Western District of
Michigan: Alger, Allegan,
Antrim, Baraga, Barry,
Benzie, Berrien, Branch,
Calhoun, Cass, Charlevioux,
Chippewa, Clinton, Delta,
Dickinson, Eaton, Emmet,
Gorgebic, Grand Traverse,
Hillsdale, Houghton,
Ingham, Ionia, Iron,
Kalamazoo, Kalkaska, Kent,
Keweenaw, Lake, Leelanau,
Luce, Mackinac, Mainistee,
Marquette, Mason, Mecosta,
Menominee, Missaukee,
Montcalm, Muskegon,
Newaygo, Oceana,
Ontonagon, Osceola, Ottawa,
Saint Joseph, Schoolcraft,
Van Buren, Wexford

United States District Court
Western District of Michigan
399 Federal BuildingilO
Michigan St. NW
Grand Rapids, MI 49503

MINNESOTA (8th Circuit)

District of Minnesota 202
U.S. Courthouse
300 S. 4th Street
Minneapolis, MN 55415

MISSISSIPPI (5th Circuit)

Northern District of
Mississippi
Aberdeen Division: Alcorn,
Attala, Chickasaw, Choctaw,
Clay, Itawamba, Lee,
Lowndes, Monroe,
Oktibbeha, Prentiss,
Tismomingo, Winston

Room 310 Federal Building
301 West Commerce
Street P.O. Box 704
Aberdeen, Mississippi 39730

Greenville Division: Carroll,
Humphreys, Leflore,
Sunflower, Washington

U.S. District Court
305 Main Street, Room 329
Greenville, Mississippi
38701-4006

Delta Division: Bolivar,
Coahoma, DeSoto, Panola,
Quitman, Tallahatchie, Tate,
Tunica

Western Division: Benton,
Calhoun, Grenada, Lafayette,
Marshall, Montgomery,
Pnotoc, Tippah, Union,
Webster, Yalobusha

Room 369 Federal Building
911 Jackson Avenue
Oxford, MS 38655

Southern District of
Mississippi: Adams, Amite,
Claiborne, Clarke, Copiah,
Covington, Forrest, Franklin,
George, Greene, Hancock,
Harrison, Hinds, Holmes,
Issaquena, Jackson,
Jasper, Jefferson, Jefferson
Davis, Jones, Kemper,

Lamar, Lauderdale,
Lawrence, Leake, Lincoln,
Madison, Marion, Nashoba,
Newton, Noxubee, Pearl
River, Perry, Pike, Rankin,
Scott, Sharkey, Simpson,
Smith, Stone, Waithall,
Warren, Wayne, Wilkinson,
Yazoo

U.S. District Court
245 East Capitol Street Suite
316
Jackson, MS 39201

MISSOURI (8th Circuit)

Eastern District of Missouri
Eastern Division: Crawford,
Dent, Franklin, Gasconade,
Iron, Jefferson, Lincoln,
Manes, Phelps, Saint
Charles, Saint Francois, Saint
Genevieve, Saint Louis,
Warren, Washington, City of
St. Louis,

Northern Division: Adair,
Audrain, Chariton, Clark,
Knox, Lewis, Linn, Marion,
Monroe, Montgomery, Pike,
Ralls, Randolph, Schuyler,
Scotland, Shelby

Thomas F. Eagleton
Courthouse
111 South 10th Street, Suite
3,300
St. Louis, MO 63102

Southeastern Division:
Bollinger, Butler, Cape

Girardeau, Carter, Dunklin,
Madison, Mississippi, New
Madrid, Pemiscot, Perry,
Reynolds, Ripley, Scott,
Shannon, Stoddard, Wayne

U.S. Courthouse
339 Broadway
Cape Girardeau, MO 63701

Western District of Missouri:
Andrew, Atchison, Barry,
Barton, Bates, Benton,
Boone, Buchanan, Caldwell,
Callaway, Camden, Carroll,
Cass, Cedar, Christian, Clay,
Clinton, Cole, Copper, Dade,
Dallas, Daviess, Dekalb,
Douglas, Gentry, Greene,
Grundy, Harrison, Henry,
Hickory, Holt, Howard,
Howell, Jackson, Jasper,
Johnson, Laclede, Lafayette,
Lawrence, Livingston,
McDonald, Mercer, Miller,
Moniteau, Morgan, Newton,
Nodaway, Oregon, Osage,
Ozark, Pettis, Platte, P1k,
Pulaski, Putnam, Ray, Saint
Clair, Saline, Stone, Sullivan,
Taney, Texas, Vernon,
Webster, Worth, Wright,
Charles Evans Whittaker

Courthouse
400 E. 9th Street
Kansas City, Missouri 64106

MONTANA (9th Ciruit)

District of Montana

Federal Building, Room
5405
316 North 26th Street
Billings, MT 59101

NEBRASKA (8th Circuit)

District of Nebraska: Adams,
Antelope, Arthur, Banner,
Blaine, Boone, Box Butte,
Boyd, Brown, Buffalo Burt,
Butler, Cass, Cedar, Chase,
Cherry, Cheyenne, Clay,
Colfax, Cumming, Custer,
Dakota, Dawes, Dawson,
Deuel, Dixon, Dudny,
Fillmore, Franklin, Frontier,
Furnas, Gage, Garden,
Garfield, Gosper, Greeley,
Hall, Hamilton, Harlan,
Hayes, Hitchcock, Holt,
Hooker, Howard, Jefferson,
Johnson, Kearney, Keith,
Keya Paha, Kimball, Knox,
Lancaster, Lincoln, Logan,
Loup, Madison, McPherson,
Merrick, Morrill, Nance,
Nemaha, Nuckolls, otoe,
Pawnee, Phelps, Pierce,
Platte, Polk, Red Willow,
Richardson, Rock, Saline,
Saunders, Scotts Bluff,
Seward, Sheridan, Sherman,
Sioux, Stanton, Thayer,
Thomas, Thurston, Valley,
Wayne, Webster, Wheeler,

York Clerk of the Court
U.S. District court -
Nebraska
P.O. Box 83468
Lincoln, NE 68501 - 3468

NEVADA (9th Circuit)

District of Nevada: Carson
City, Churchill, Douglas,
Elko, Eureka, Humboldt,
Lander, Lyon, Mineral,
Pershing, Storey, Washoe,
White Pine

Clerk of the Court
U.S. District Court of
Nevada Northern Division
400 S. Virginia St.
Reno, NV 89501

NEW HAMPSHIRE (1st Circuit)

District of New Hampshire
Clerk of the Court
U.S. District Court - New
Hampshire Warren B.
Rudman U.S. Courthouse
55 Pleasant Street, Room 110
Concord, NH 03301-3941

NEW JERSEY (3d Circuit)

District of New Jersey
Martin Luther King U.S.
Courthouse 50 Walnut
Street, Room 4015
Newark, NJ 07101

NEW MEXICO (10th Circuit)

District of New Mexico
U.S. District Courthouse
33 Lomas N.W.
Albuquerque, NM 87102

NEW YORK (2d Circuit)

Northern District of New York: Albany, Broome, Cayuga, Chenango, Clinton, Columbia, Cortland, Delaware, Essex, Franklin, Fulton, Greene, Hamilton, Herkimer, Jefferson, Lewis, Madison, Montgomery, Oneida, Onondaga, Oswego, Otsesgo, Rensselaer, Saratoga, Schenectady, Schoharie, St. Lawrence, Tioga, Tompkins, Ulster, Warren, Washington

United States District Court for the Northern District of New York U.S. Courthouse & Federal Bldg.
P.O. Box 7367
100 South Clinton Street
Syracuse, NY 13261-7367

Southern District of New York: Bronx, Dutchess, New York, Orange, Putnam, Rockland, Sullivan, Westchester

United States District Court of the Southern District of New York Daniel Patrick Moynihan United States Courthouse
500 Pearl Street
New York, NY 10007-1312

Eastern District of New York: Kings, Nassau, Queens, Richmond, Suffolk

U.S. District Court
Eastern District of New York
225 Cadman Plaza East
Brooklyn, New York 11201

Western District of New York
Buffalo Division: Allegany, Cattaraugus, Chautauqua, Erie, Genesee, Niagara, Orleans, Wyoming

United States District Court for the Western Division of New York Office of the Clerk
304 united States Courthouse
68 Court Street
Buffalo, New York 14202

74 Rochester Division: Livingston, Monroe, Ontario, Schuyler, Seneca, Steuben, Wayne, Yates

United States District Court for the Western Division of New York Office of the Clerk
2120 United States Courthouse
100 State Street
Rochester, New York 14614-1387

NORTH CAROLINA (4th Circuit)

Eastern District of North Caroline: Beaufort, Betrie, Bladen, Brunswick, Camden, Carteret, Chowan, Columbus, Craven, Cumberland, Cerrituck, Dare, Duplin, Edgecombe, Franklin, Gates, Granville, Greene, Halifax, Harnett, Hertford, Hyde, Johnston, Jones, Lenoir, Martin, Nash, New Hanover, Northampton, Onslow, Pamlico, Pasquotank, Pender, Perquimans, Pitt, Robeson, Sampson, Tyrell, Vance, Wake, Warren, Washington, Wayne, Wilson

Clerk of the Court
United States District Court
for the Eastern
District of North Carolina
Terry Sanford Federal
Building and Courthouse
310 New Bern Avenue
Raleigh, North Carolina
27601

Middle District of North Caroline: Alamance, Alleghany, Ashe, Cabarrus, Caswell, Chatham, Davidson, Davie, Durham, Forsyth, Guilford, Hoke, Lee, Montgomery, Moore, Orange, Person, Randolph, Richmond, Rockingham, Rowan, Scotland, Stanly, Stokes, Surry, Watauga, Yadkin

Office of the Clerk, U.S.
District Court Middle
District of North Carolina
P.O. Box 2708
Greensboro, NC 27402-2708

Western District of North
Carolina
Asheville Division:
Haywood Madison, Yancey, Watuaga, Avery, Buncombe, McDowell, Burke, Transylvania, Henderson, Polk, Rutherford, Cleveland, Cherokee, Clay, Graham, Jackson, Macon, Swain

U.S. District Court
100 Otis St.
Ashevile, NC 28801

Charlotte Division: Gaston, Mecklenburg, Union, Anson

U.S. District Court Room
212
401 W. Trade St.
Charlotte, NC 28202

Statesville Division:
Watauga, Ashe, Alleghany, Caldwell, Wilkes, Alexander, Iredell, Catawba, Lincoln

U.S. District Court 220 W.
Broad St.
Statesville, NC 28677

NORTH DAKOTA (8th Circuit) District of North Dakota

U.S. District Court
220 East Rosse Avenue
P.O. Box 1193
Bismarck, ND 58502

**NORTHERN MARIANA
ISLANDS (9th Circuit)**

District for the Northern
Marina Islands
U.S. District Court for the
Northern Mariana Islands
2nd Floor, Horiguchi
Building, Garapan
P.O. Box 500687
Saipan, MP 96950 USA

OHIO (6th Circuit)

Northern District of Ohio
Eastern Division: Ashland,
Ashtabula, Carroll,
Clumbiana, Crawford,
Cuyahog, Geauga, Holmes,
Lake, Lorain, Mahoning,
Medina, Portage, Richland,
Stark, Summit, Trumbull,
Tuscarawas, Wayne

U.S. District Court for the
Northern District of Ohio 2
South Main Street
Akron, OII 44308

Western Division: Allen,
Auglaize, Defiance, Erie,
Fulton, Hancock, Hardin,
Henry, Huron, Lucas, Mario,
Mercer, Ottawa, Paulding,
Putnam, Sandusky, Seneca,
Van Wert, Williams, Wood,
Wyandot

United States District Court
for the Northern District of
Ohio 1716 Spielbusch
Avenue
Toledo, OH 43624

Southern District of Ohio:
Athens, Belmont,
Coschocton, Delaware,
Fairfield, Fayette, Franklin,
Gallia, Guernsey, Harrison,
Hocking, Jackson, Jefferson,
Knox, Licking, Logan,
Madison, Meigs, Monroe,
Morgan, Morrow,
Muskingum, Noble, Perry,
Pickaway, Pike, Ross, Union,
Vinton, Washington

United States District Court
for the Southern
District of Ohio Joseph P.
Kinneary U.S. Courthouse,
Room 260
85 Marconi Boulevard
Comumbus, OH 43215

**OKLAHOMA (10th
Circuit)**

Northern District of
Oklahoma: Craig, Creek,
Delaware, Mayes, Nowata,
Osage, Ottawa, Pawnee,
Rogers, Tulsa, Washington

United States District Court
for the Northern District of
Oklahoma 333 W. 4th St.
Room 411
Tulsa, OK 74103

Eastern District of
Oklahoma: Adair, Atoka,
Bryan, Carter, Cherokee,
Choctaw, Coal, Haskell,
Hughes, Johnston, Latimer,
Le Flore, Love, Marshall,
McCurtain, McIntosh,
Murray, Muskogee,
Okfuskee, Okmulgee,
Pittsburg, Ponotoc,
Pushmataha, Seminole,
Sequoyah, Wagoner

United States District Court
for the Eastern District of
Ohio 101 N. 5th Street
P.O. Box 607
Muskogee, OK 74402-0607

Western District of
Oklahoma: Alfalfa, Beaver,
Beckham, Blaine, Caddo,
Canadian, Cimarron,
Cleveland, Comanche,
Cotton, Custer, Dewey, Ellis,
Garfield, Garvin, Grady,
Grant,
Greer, Harmon, Harper,
Jackson, Jefferson, Kay,
Kingfisher, Kiowa, Lincoln,
Logan, Major, McClain,
Noble, Oklahoma, Payne,
Pottawatomie, Roger Mills,
Stephens, Texas, Tillman,
Washita, Woods, Woodward

United States District Court
for the Western District of
Oklahoma
200 NW 4th Street, Room
1210

Oklahoma City, OK 73102

OREGON (9th Circuit)

District of Oregon
Portland Division: Baker,
Clackamas, Clatsop,
Columbia, Crook, Gilliam,
Grant, Harney, Hood River,
Jefferson, Malheur, Morrow,
Multnomah, Pik, Sherman,
Tillamook, Umatilla, Union,
Wallowa, Wasco,
Washington, Wheeler,
Yamhill

United States District Court
for the District of Oregon
Mark 0. Hatfield U.S.
Courthouse, Room 740
1000 S.W. Third Avenue
Portland, OR 97204

Eugene Division: Benton,
Coos, Deschutes, Douglas,
Lane, Lincoln, Linn, Marion

United States District Court
for the District of Oregon
United States Courthouse,
Room 100
211 E. Seventh Avenue
Eugene, OR 97401

Medford Division: Curry,
Jackson, Josephine, Klamath,
Lake

United States District Court
for the District of Oregon
James A. Redden U.S.
Courthouse, Room 213

310 W. Sixth Avenue
Medford, OR 97501

PENNSYLVANIA (3d Circuit)

Eastern District of
Pennsylvania: Berks, Bucks,
Chester, Delaware,
Lancaster, Lehigh,
Montgomery, Northampton,
Philadelphia

United States District Court
for the Eastern District of
Pennsylvania U.S.
Courthouse 601 Market
Street, Room 2609
Philadelphia, PA 19106-1797

Middle District of
Pennsylvania: Adams,
Bradford, Cameron, Carbon,
Centre, Clinton, Columbia,
Cumberland, Dauphin.
Franklin, Fulton.
Huntingdon, Juniata,
Lackawanna, Lebanon,
Luzerne, Lycoming, Mifflin,
Monroe, Montour,
Northumberland, Perry, Pike,
Potter, Schuylkill, Snyder,
Sullivan, Susquehanna,
Tioga, Union, Wayne,
Wyoming, York

United States District Court
for the Middle District of
Pennsylvania William J,
Nealon
Federal Building & U.S.
Courthouse

235 N. Washington Ave.
P.O. Box 1148
Scranton, PA 18501

Western District of
Pennsylvania: Allegheny,
Armstrong, Beaver, Butler,
Clarion, Fayette, Greene,
Indiana, Jefferson Lawrence,
Mercer, Washington,
Westmoreland

United States District Court
for the Western District of
Pennsylvania
P.O. Box 1805
Pittsburgh, PA 15230

PUERTO RICO (1st Circuit)

District of Puerto Rico
Clemente Ruiz-Nazario U.S.
Courthouse &
Federico Degetau Federal
Building
150 Carlos Chardon Street
Hato Rey, PR 00918

RHODE ISLAND (1st Circuit)

District of Rhode Island
United States District Court
for the District of Rhode
Island
One Exchange Terrace
Federal Building and
Courthouse
Providence, RI 02903

SOUTH CAROLINA (4th Circuit)

District of South Carolina:
Aiken, Barnwell, Allendale,
Kershaw, Lee, Sumter,
Richland, Lexington, Aiken,
Barnwell, Allendale, York,
Chester, Lancaster, Fairfield

United States District Court
for the District of South
Carolina Matthew J. Perry,
Jr. Courthouse
901 Richland Street
Columbia, South Carolina
29201

SOUTH DAKOTA (8th Circuit)

District of South Dakota
United States District Court
for the District of South
Dakota Rm 128 United
States Courthouse
400 S. Phillips Avenue
Sioux Falls, SD 57104

TENNESSEE (6th Circuit)

Eastern District of Tennessee
Greeneville Division: Carter,
Cocke, Greene, Hamblen,
Hancock, Hawkins, Johnson,
Sullivan, Unicoi,
Washington

United States District Court
for the Eastern District of
Tennessee

220 West Depot Street, Suite
200
Greeneville, TN 37743

Knoxville Division:
Anderson, Blunt, Campbell,
Claiborne, Grainger,
Jefferson, Knox, Loudon,
Monroe, Morgan, Roane,
Scott, Sevier, Union

United States District Court
for the Eastern
District of Tennessee
800 Market Street, Suite 130
Knoxville, TN 37902

Chattanooga Division:
Bledsoe, Bradley, Hamilton,
McMinn, Marion, Meigs,
Polk, Rhea, Sequatchie

United States District Court
for the Eastern District of
Tennessee
900 Georgia Avenue
Chattanooga, TN 37402

Winchester Division:
Bedford, Coffee, Granklin,
Grundy, Lincoln, Moore,
Warren, Van Buren

United States District Court
for the Eastern District of
Tennessee
200 South Jefferson Street
Winchester, TN 37398

Middle District of
Tennessee: Cannon,
Cheatham, Clay,

Cumberland, Davidson, De
Kalb, Dickson, Fentress,
Giles, Hickman, Houston,
Humphreys, Jackson,
Lawrence, Lewis, Macon,
Marshall, Maury,
Montgomery, Overton,
Pickett, Putnam, Robertson,
Rutherford, Smith, Stewart,
Sumner, Trousdale, Wayne,
White, Williamson, Wilson
United States District Court
for the Middle

District of Tennessee
Nashville Clerk's Office
801 Broadway, Room 800
Nashville, TN 37203

Western District of
Tennessee: Dyer, Fayette,
Lauderdale, Shelby, Tipton
United States

TEXAS

Galveston Division:
Brazoria, Chambers,
Galveston, Matagorda

United States District Court
for the Southern District of
Texas
P.O. Box 2300
Galveston, TX 77550

Houston Division: Austin,
Brazos, Colorado, Fayette,
Fort Bend, Grimes, Harris
Madison, Montgomery, San
Jacinto, Walker, Wailer,
Wharton

United States District Court
for the Southern District of
Texas P.O. Box 61010
Houston, TX 77002

Laredo Division: Jim Hogg,
LaSalle, McMullen, Webb,
Zapata

United States District Court
for the Southern District of
Texas
P.O. Box 597
Laredo, TX 78042

McAllen Division: Hidalgo,
Starr

United States District Court
for the Southern District of
Texas 1701 West Business
Highway
Suite 1011
McAllen, Tx 78501

Victoria Division: Calhoun,
De Witt, Goliad, Jackson,
Lavaca, Refugio, Victoria

United States District Court
for the Southern District of
Texas
P.O. Box 1638
Victoria, TX 77902

Western District of Texas:
Bastrop, Blanco, Burleson,
Burnet, Caldwell, Gillespie,
Hays, Kinbie, Lampasas,
Lee, Llano, Mason,
McCulloch, San Saba,

119

Travis, Washington, Williamson

United States District Court for the Western District of Texas U.S. District Clerk's Office
200 West 8th St., Room 130
Austin, Texas 78701

United States District Court for the Western District of Texas U.S. District Clerk's Office
511 East San Antonio Ave., Room 350
El Paso, Texas 79901

UTAH (10th Circuit)

District of Utah
United States District Court for the District of Utah 350 South Main Street
Salt Lake City, UT 84101

VERMONT (2d Circuit)

District of Vermont
United States District Court for the District of Vermont
P.O. Box 945
Burlington, VT 05402-0945

VIRGIN ISLANDS (3d Circuit)

District of the Virgin Islands
United States District Court for the District of the Virgin Islands

5500 Veterans Drive, Room 310
St. Thomas, VI 00802

VIRGINIA (4th Circuit)

Eastern District of Virginia: Alexandria, Loudoun, Fairfax, Fauquier, Arlington, Prince William, Stafford

U.S. District Court, Eastern District of Virginia Albert V. Bryan U.S. Courthouse
401 Courthouse Square
Alexandria, VA 22314

Western District of Virginia: Bristol, Buchanan, Russel, Smyth, Tazewell, Washington

U.S. District Court, Western District of Virginia 180 W. Main Street, Room 104
Abingdon, VA 24210

WASHINGTON (9th Circuit)

Eastern District of Washington: Adams, Asotin, Benton, Chelan, Columbia, Douglas, Ferry, Franklin, Garfield, Grant, Kittitas, Klickitat, Lincoln, Okanogan, Pend Oreille, Spokane, Stevens, Walla Walls, Yakima

U.S. District Court, Eastern District of Washington Clerk of the Court

Eastern District of Texas

Beaumont Division: Hardin, Jasper, Jefferson, Liberty, Newton, Orange

United States District Court for the Eastern District of Texas
300 Willow Street
Beaumont, TX 77701

Marshall Division: Camp, Cass, Harrison, Marion, Morris, Upshur

United States District Court for the Eastern District of Texas U.S. District Clerk
100 E. Houston, Room 125
Marshall, TX 75670

Sherman Division: Collin, Cooke, Denton, Grayson, Delta, Fannin, Hopkins, Lamar

United States District Court for the Eastern District of Texas U.S. District Clerk
101 E. Pecan St. Room 112
Sherman, TX 75090

Texarkana Division: Bowie, Franklin, Titus, Red River

United States District Court for the Eastern District of Texas
U.S. District Clerk
301 U.S. Courthouse 500 Stateline Avenue Texarkana, TX 75501

Tyler Division: Anderson, Cherokee, Gregg, Henderson, Panola, Rains, Rusk, Smith, Van Zandt, Wood

United States District Court for the Eastern District of Texas 211 W. Ferguson Room 106
Tyler, TX 75702

Lufkin Division: Angelina, Houston, Nacogdoches, Polk, Sabine, San Augustine, Shelby, Trinity, Tyler

United States District Court for the Eastern District of Texas 104 N. Third Street
Lufkin, TX 75901

Southern District of Texas
Brownsville Division: Cameron, Willacy

United States District Court for the Southern District of Texas
600 East Harrison Street, Room 101
Brownsville, TX 78520

121

Corpus Christi Division: Aransas, Bee, Brooks, Duval, Jim Wells, Kennedy, Kleberg, Live Oak, Nueces, San Patricio

United States District Court for the Southern District of Texas 1133 North Shoreline, Blvd.
Room 242, Federal Building 167 North Main Street Memphis, TN 38103

TEXAS (5th Circuit)

Northern District of Texas Abilene Division: Jones, Nolan, Stephens, Throckmorton, Fisher, Haskell, Howard, Shackelford, Stonewall, Taylor, Callahan, Eastland, Mitchell

United States District Court for the Northern District of Texas 341 Pine Street, 2008 Abilene, TX 79601

Amarillo Division: Carson, Deaf Smith, Gray, Hutchinson, Swisher, Armstrong, Brisco, Castro, Dallam, Hartley, Moore, Ochiltree, Parmer, Roberts, Childress, Donley, Hall, Lipscomb, Oldham, Potter, Wheeler, Collingsworth, Hansford, Hemphill, Randall, Sherman

United States District Court for the Northern District of Texas 205 E. Fifth Street, 133
Amarillo, TX 79101-1559

Dallas Division: Ellis, Kaufman, Dallas, Rockwall, Hunt, Johnson, Navarro

United States District Court for the Northern District of Texas 1100 Commerce St., 1452
Dallas, TX 75242

Fort Worth Division: Comanche, Perker, Erath, Hood, Tarrant, Wise, Jack, Palo Pinto
United States District Court for the Northern

District of Texas
501 West 10th Street, 310
Fort Worth, TX 76102-3673

Lubbock Division: Borden, Cochran, Crosby, Hockley, Lynn, Dickens, Gaines, Hale, Lamb, Scurry, Bailey, Garza, Kent, Motley, Yoakum, Dawson, Floyd, Lubbock, Terry

United States District Court for the Northern District of Texas 1205 Texas Avenue, C-221
Lubbock, TX 79401-4091

San Angelo Division:
Reagan, Schleicher, Coke,
Concho, Irion, Menard,
Sterling, Tom Green, Brown,
Coleman, Mills, Crockett,
Glasscock, Runnels, Sutton

United States District Court
for the Northern District of
Texas 33 E. Twohig Street,
202
San Angelo, TX 76903-6451

Wichita Falls Division:
Archer, Hardeman, Knox,
Montague, Wilbarger, Cottle,
Baylor, Clay, King, Wichita,
Young

United States District Court
for the Northern
District of Texas
1000 Lamar Street, 203
Wichita Falls, TX 76301
P.O. Box 1493
Spokane, WA 99210

Western District of
Washington: Clallam, Clark,
Cowlitz, Grays Harbor,
Jefferson, Kitsap, Lewis,
Mason, Pacific, Pierce,
Skamania, Thurston,
Wahkiakum

U.S. District Court, Western
District of Washington 1717
Pacific Avenue
Tacoma, WA 98402

**WEST VIRGINIA (4th
Circuit)**

Northern District of West
Virginia: Brooke, Hancock,
Marshall, Ohio, Wetzel

U.S. District Court, Northern
District of West Virginia
1125 Chaplin Street
Wheeling, WV 26003

Southern District of West
Virginia
Beckley Division: Fayette,
Greenbrier, Summers,
Raleigh, Wyoming

U.S. District Court, Southern
District of West Virginia
Federal Building and
Courthouse
P.O. Drawer 5009
Beckley, WV 25801

Bluefield Division: Mercer,
Monroe, McDowell

U.S. District Court, Southern
District of West Virginia
P.O. Box 4128
Bluefield, WV 24701

Charleston Division: Boone,
Clay, Jackson, Kanawha,
Lincoln, Logan, Mingo,
Nicholas, Putnam, Roane

U.S. District Court, Southern
District of West Virginia
U.S. Courthouse
P.O. Box 2546
Charleston, WV 25329

Huntington Division: Cabell,
Mason, Wayne

U.S. District Court, Southern
District of West Virginia
Sidney L. Christie Federal
Building
P.O. Box 1570
Huntington, WV 25716
Parkersburg Division: Wirt,
Wood

U.S. District Court, Southern
District of West Virginia
Federal Building and
Courthouse
425 Juliana Street, Room
5102
Parkersburg, WV 26102

WISCONSIN (7th Circuit)

Eastern District of
Wisconsin: Brown, Calumet,
Dodge, Door, Florence, Fond
du Lac, Forest, Green Lake,
Kenosha, Kewaunee,
Langlade, Manitowoc,
Marinette, Marquette,
Menominee, Milwaukee,
Oconto, Outagamie,
Ozaukee, Racine, Shawano,
Sheboygan, Walworth,
Washington, Waukesha,
Waupaca, Waushara,
Winnebago

U.S. District Court, Eastern
District of Wisconsin
362 U.S. Courthouse
517 East Wisconsin Avenue
Milwaukee, WI 53202

Western District of
Wisconsin: Adams, Ashland,
Barron, Bayfield, Buffalo,
Burnett, Chippewa, Clark,
Columbia, Crawford, Dane,
Douglas, Dunn, Eau Claire,
Grant, Green, Iowa, Iron,
Jackson, Jefferson, Juneau,
La Crosse, Lafayette,
Lincoln, Marathon, Monroe,
Oneida, pepin, Pierce, Polk,
Portage, Price, Richland,
Rock, Rusk, Sauk, St. Croix,
Sawyer, Taylor,
Trempealeau, Vernon, Villas,
Washburn, Wood

U.S. District Court Western
District of Wisconsin 120
North Henry Street, Room
320
P.O. Box 432
Madison, WI 53701-0432

WYOMING (10th Circuit)

District of Wyoming
U.S. District Court, District
of Wyoming
2120 Capitol Ave., 2nd Floor
Cheyenne, WY 82001-3658

THE CELL BLOCK
BOOK SUMMARIES

MIKE ENEMIGO is the new prison/street art sensation who has written and published several books. He is inspired by emotion; hope; pain; dreams and nightmares. He physically lives somewhere in a California prison cell where he works relentlessly creating his next piece. His mind and soul are elsewhere; seeing, studying, learning, and drawing inspiration to tear down suppressive walls and inspire the culture by pushing artistic boundaries.

THE CELL BLOCK is an independent multimedia company with the objective of accurately conveying the prison/street experience with the credibility and honesty that only one who has lived it can deliver, through literature and other arts, and to entertain and enlighten while doing so. Everything published by The Cell Block has been created by a prisoner, while in a prison cell.

THE BEST RESOURCE DIRECTORY FOR PRISONERS, $17.95 & $5.00 S/H: This book has over 1,450 resources for prisoners! Includes: Pen-Pal Companies! Non-Nude Photo Sellers! Free Books and Other Publications! Legal Assistance! Prisoner Advocates! Prisoner Assistants! Correspondence Education! Money-Making Opportunities! Resources for Prison Writers, Poets, Artists! And much, much more! Anything you can think of doing from your prison cell, this book contains the resources to do it!

A GUIDE TO RELAPSE PREVENTION FOR PRISONERS, $15.00 & $5.00 S/H: This book provides the information and guidance that can make a real difference in the preparation of a comprehensive relapse prevention plan. Discover how to meet the parole board's expectation using these proven and practical principles. Included is a blank template and sample relapse prevention plan to assist in your preparation.

THEE ENEMY OF THE STATE (SPECIAL EDITION), $9.99 & $4.00 S/H: Experience the inspirational journey of a kid who was introduced to the art of rapping in 1993, struggled between his dream of becoming a professional rapper and the reality of the streets, and was finally offered a recording deal in 1999, only to be arrested minutes later and eventually sentenced to life in prison for murder... However, despite his harsh reality, he dedicated himself to hip-hop once again, and with resilience and determination, he sets out to prove he may just be one of the dopest rhyme writers/spitters ever .... At this point, it becomes deeper than rap .... Welcome to a preview of the greatest story you never heard.

LOST ANGELS: $15.00 & $5.00: David Rodrigo was a child who belonged to no world; rejected for his mixed heritage by most of his family and raised by an outcast uncle in the mean streets of East L.A. Chance cast him into a far darker and more devious pit of intrigue that stretched from the barest gutters to the halls of power in the great city. Now, to survive the clash of lethal forces arrayed about him, and to protect those he loves, he has only two allies; his quick wits, and the flashing blade that earned young David the street name, Viper.

LOYALTY AND BETRAYAL DELUXE EDITION, $19.99 & $7.00 S/H: Chunky was an associate of and soldier for the notorious Mexican Mafia – La Eme. That is, of course, until he was betrayed by those, he was most loyal to. Then he vowed to become their worst enemy. And though they've attempted to kill him numerous times, he still to this day is running around making a mockery of their organization .... This is the story of how it all began.

MONEY IZ THE MOTIVE: SPECIAL 2-IN-1 EDITION, $19.99 & $7.00 S/H: Like most kids growing up in the hood, Kano has a dream of going from rags to riches. But when his plan to get fast money by robbing the local "mom and pop" shop goes wrong, he quickly finds himself sentenced to serious prison time. Follow Kano as he is schooled to the ways of the game by some of the most respected OGs whoever did it; then is set free and given the resources to put his schooling into action and build the ultimate hood empire...

DEVILS & DEMONS: PART 1, $15.00 & $5.00 S/H: When Talton leaves the West Coast to set up shop in Florida he meets the female version of himself: A drug dealing murderess with psychological issues. A whirlwind of sex, money and murder inevitably ensues and Talton finds himself on the run from the law with nowhere to turn to. When his team from home finds out he's in trouble, they get on a plane heading south...

DEVILS & DEMONS: PART 2, $15.00 & $5.00 S/H: The Game is bitter-sweet for Talton, aka Gangsta. The same West Coast Clique who came to his aid ended up putting bullets into the chest of the woman he had fallen in love with. After leaving his ride or die in a puddle of her own blood, Talton finds himself on a flight back to Oak Park, the neighborhood where it all started...

DEVILS & DEMONS: PART 3, $15.00 & $5.00 S/H: Talton is on the road to retribution for the murder of the love of his life. Dante and his crew of killers are on a path of no return. This urban classic is based on real-life West Coast underworld politics. See what happens when a group of YG's find themselves in the midst of real underworld demons...

DEVILS & DEMONS: PART 4, $15.00 & $5.00 S/H: After waking up from a coma, Alize has locked herself away from the rest of the world. When her sister Brittany and their friend finally take her on a girl's night out, she meets Luck – a drug dealing womanizer.

FREAKY TALES, $15.00 & $5.00 S/H: *Freaky Tales* is the first book in a brand-new erotic series. King Guru, author of the *Devils & Demons* books, has put together a collection of sexy short stories and memoirs. In true TCB fashion, all of the erotic tales included in this book have been loosely based on true accounts told to, or experienced by the author.

THE ART & POWER OF LETTER WRITING FOR PRISONERS: DELUXE EDITION $19.99 & $7.00 S/H: When locked inside a prison cell, being able to write well is the most powerful skill you can have! Learn how to increase your power by writing high-quality personal and formal letters! Includes letter templates, pen-pal website strategies, punctuation guide and more!

THE PRISON MANUAL: $24.99 & $7.00 S/H: *The Prison Manual* is your all-in-one book on how to not only survive the rough terrain of the American prison system, but use it to your advantage so you can THRIVE from it! How to Use Your Prison Time to YOUR Advantage; How to Write Letters that Will Give You Maximum Effectiveness; Workout and Physical Health Secrets that Will Keep You as FIT as Possible; The Psychological impact of incarceration and How to Maintain Your MAXIMUM Level of Mental Health; Prison Art Techniques; Fulfilling Food Recipes; Parole Preparation Strategies and much, MUCH more!

GET OUT, STAY OUT!, $16.95 & $5.00 S/H: This book should be in the hands of everyone in a prison cell. It reveals a challenging but clear course for overcoming the obstacles that stand between prisoners and their freedom. For those behind bars, one goal outshines all others: GETTING OUT! After being released, that goal then shifts to STAYING OUT! This book will help prisoners do both. It has been masterfully constructed into five parts that will help prisoners maximize focus while they strive to accomplish whichever goal is at hand.

MOB$TAR MONEY, $12.00 & $4.00 S/H: After Trey's mother is sent to prison for 75 years to life, he and his little brother are moved from their home in Sacramento, California, to his grandmother's house in Stockton, California where he is forced to find his way in life and become a man on his own in the city's grimy streets. One day, on his way home from the local corner store, Trey has a rough encounter with the neighborhood bully. Luckily, that's when Tyson, a member of the MOBTAR, a local "get money" gang comes to his aid. The two kids quickly become friends, and it doesn't take long before Trey is embraced into the notorious MOB$TAR money gang, which opens the door to an adventure full of sex, money, murder and mayhem that will change his life forever... You will never guess how this story ends!

BLOCK MONEY, $12.00 & $4.00 S/H: Beast, a young thug from the grimy streets of central Stockton, California lives The Block; breathes The Block; and has committed himself to bleed The Block for all it's worth until his very last breath. Then, one day, he meets Nadia; a stripper at the local club who piques his curiosity with her beauty, quick-witted intellect and rider qualities. The problem? She has a man – Esco – a local kingpin with money and power. It doesn't take long, however, before a devious plot is hatched to pull off a heist worth an indeterminable amount of money. Following the acts of treachery, deception and betrayal are twists and turns and a bloody war that will leave you speechless!

HOW TO HUSTLE AND WIN: SEX, MONEY, MURDER EDITION $15.00 & $5.00 S/H: *How To Hu$tle and Win: Sex, Money, Murder Edition* is the grittiest, underground self-help manual for the 21st century street entrepreneur in print. Never has there been such a book written for today's gangsters, goons and go-getters. This self-help handbook is an absolute must-have for anyone who is actively connected to the streets.

RAW LAW: YOUR RIGHTS, & HOW TO SUE WHEN THEY ARE VIOLATED! $15.00 & $5.00 S/H: *Raw Law For Prisoners* is a clear and concise guide for prisoners and their advocates to understanding civil rights laws guaranteed to prisoners under the US Constitution, and how to successfully file a lawsuit when those rights have been violated! From initial complaint to trial, this book will take you through the entire process, step by step, in simple, easy-to-understand terms. Also included are several examples where prisoners have sued prison officials successfully, resulting in changes of unjust rules and regulations and recourse for rights violations, oftentimes resulting in rewards of thousands, even millions of dollars in damages! If you feel your rights have been violated, don't lash out at guards, which is usually ineffective and only makes matters worse. Instead, defend yourself successfully by using the legal system, and getting the power of the courts on your side!

HOW TO WRITE URBAN BOOKS FOR MONEY & FAME: $16.95 & $5.00 S/H: Inside this book you will learn the true story of how Mike Enemigo and King Guru have received money and fame from inside their prison cells by writing urban books; the secrets to writing hood classics so you, too, can be caked up and famous; proper punctuation using hood examples; and resources you can use to achieve your money motivated ambitions! If you're a prisoner who want to write urban novels for money and fame, this must-have manual will give you all the game!

PRETTY GIRLS LOVE BAD BOYS: AN INMATE'S GUIDE TO GETTING GIRLS: $15.00 & $5.00 S/H: Tired of the same, boring, cliché pen pal books that don't tell you what you really need to know? If so, this book is for you! Anything you need to know on the art of long and short distance seduction is included within these pages! Not only does it give you the science of attracting pen pals from websites, it also includes psychological profiles and instructions on how to seduce any woman you set your sights on! Includes interviews of women who have fallen in love with prisoners, bios for pen pal ads, pre-written love letters, romantic poems, love-song lyrics, jokes and much, much more! This book is the ultimate guide – a must-have for any prisoner who refuses to let prison walls affect their MAC'n.

THE LADIES WHO LOVE PRISONERS, $15.00 & $5.00 S/H: New Special Report reveals the secrets of real women who have fallen in love with prisoners, regardless of crime, sentence, or location. This info will give you a HUGE advantage in getting girls from prison.

THE MILLIONAIRE PRISONER: PART 1, $16.95 & $5.00 S/H

THE MILLIONAIRE PRISONER: PART 2, $16.95 & $5.00 S/H

THE MILLIONAIRE PRISONER: SPECIAL 2-IN-1 EDITION, $24.99 & $7.00 S/H: Why wait until you get out of prison to achieve your dreams? Here's a blueprint that you can use to become successful! *The Millionaire Prisoner* is your complete reference to overcoming any obstacle in prison. You won't be able to put it down! With this book you will discover the secrets to: Making money from your cell! Obtain FREE money for correspondence courses! Become an expert on any topic! Develop the habits of the rich! Network with celebrities! Set up your own website! Market your products, ideas and services! Successfully use prison pen pal websites! All of this and much, much more! This book has enabled thousands of prisoners to succeed and it will show you the way also!

THE MILLIONAIRE PRISONER 3: SUCCESS UNIVERSITY, $16.95 & $5 S/H: Why wait until you get out of prison to achieve your dreams? Here's a new-look blueprint that you can use to be successful! *The Millionaire Prisoner 3* contains advanced strategies to overcoming any obstacle in prison. You won't be able to put it down!

THE MILLIONAIRE PRISONER 4: PEN PAL MASTERY, $16.95 & $5 S/H: Tired of subpar results? Here's a master blueprint that you can use to get tons of pen pals! *TMP 4: Pen Pal Mastery* is your complete roadmap to finding your one true love. You won't be able to put it down! With this book you'll DISCOVER the SECRETS to: Get FREE pen pals & which sites are best to use; successful tactics female prisoners can win with; use astrology to find love, friendship & more, build a winning social media presence. All of this and much more!

GET OUT, GET RICH: HOW TO GET PAID LEGALLY WHEN YOU GET OUT OF PRISON!, $16.95 & $5.00 S/H: Many of you are incarcerated for a money-motivated crime. But w/ today's tech & opportunities, not only is the crime-for-money risk/reward ratio not strategically wise, it's not even necessary. You can earn much more money by partaking in any one of the easy, legal hustles explained in this book, regardless of your record. Help yourself earn an honest income so you can not only make a lot of money, but say good-bye to penitentiary chances and prison forever! (Note: Many things in this book can even he done from inside prison.)

(ALSO PUBLISHED AS *HOOD MILLIONAIRE: HOW TO HUSTLE AND WIN LEGALLY!*)

THE CEO MANUAL: HOW TO START A BUSINESS WHEN YOU GET OUT OF PRISON, $16.95 & $5.00 S/H: $16.95 & $5 S/H: This new book will teach you the simplest way to start your own business when you get out of prison. Includes: Start-up Steps! The Secrets to Pulling Money from Investors! How to Manage People Effectively! How To Legally Protect Your Assets from "them"! Hundreds of resources to get you started, including a list of "loan friendly" banks! (ALSO PUBLISHED AS *CEO MANUAL: START A BUSINESS, BE A BOSS!*)

THE MONEY MANUAL: UNDERGROUND CASH SECRETS EXPOSED! 16.95 & $5.00 S/H: Becoming a millionaire is equal parts what you make, and what you don't spend – AKA save. All Millionaires and Billionaires have mastered the art of not only making money, but keeping the money they make (remember Donald Trump's tax maneuvers?), as well as establishing credit so that they are loaned money by banks and trusted with money from investors: AKA OPM – other people's money. And did you know there are millionaires and billionaires just waiting to GIVE money away? It's true! These are all very-little known secrets "they" don't want YOU to know about, but that I'm exposing in my new book!

HOOD MILLIONAIRE; HOW TO HUSTLE & WIN LEGALLY, $16.95 & $5.00 S/H: Hustlin' is a way of life in the hood. We all have money motivated ambitions, not only because we gotta eat, but because status is oftentimes determined by one's own salary.

To achieve what we consider financial success, we often invest our efforts into illicit activities – we take penitentiary chances. This leads to a life in and out of prison, sometimes death – both of which are counterproductive to gettin' money. But there's a solution to this, and I have it...

CEO MANUAL: START A BUSINESS BE A BOSS, $16.95 & $5.00 S/H: After the success of the urban-entrepreneur classic *Hood Millionaire: How To Hustle & Win Legally!*, self-made millionaires Mike Enemigo and Sav Hustle team back up to bring you the latest edition of the Hood Millionaire series – *CEO Manual: Start A Business, Be A Boss!* In this latest collection of game laying down the art of "hoodpreneurship", you will learn such things as: 5 Core Steps to Starting Your Own Business! 5 Common Launch Errors You Must Avoid! How To Write a Business Plan! How To Legally Protect Your Assets From "Them"! How To Make Your Business Fundable, Where to Get Money for Your Start-up Business, and even How to Start a Business With No Money! You will learn How to Drive Customers to Your Website, How to Maximize Marketing Dollars, Contract Secrets for the savvy boss, and much, much more! And as an added bonus, we have included over 200 Business Resources, from government agencies and small business development centers, to a secret list of small-business friendly banks that will help you get started!

PAID IN FULL: WELCOME TO DA GAME, $15.00 & $5.00 S/H. In 1983, the movie *Scarface* inspired many kids growing up in America's inner cities to turn their rags into riches by becoming cocaine kingpins. Harlem's Azie Faison was one of them. Faison would ultimately connect with Harlem's

Rich Porter and Alpo Martinez, and the trio would go on to become certified street legends of the '80s and early '90s. Years later, Dame Dash and Roc-A-Fella Films would tell their story in the based-on-actual-events movie, *Paid in Full*.

But now, we are telling the story our way – The Cell Block way – where you will get a perspective of the story that the movie did not show, ultimately learning an outcome that you did not expect.

Book one of our series, *Paid in Full: Welcome to da Game*, will give you an inside look at a key player in this story, one that is not often talked about – Lulu, the Columbian cocaine kingpin with direct ties to Pablo Escobar, who plugged Azie in with an unlimited amount of top-tier cocaine at dirt-cheap prices that helped boost the trio to neighborhood superstars and certified kingpin status... until greed, betrayal, and murder destroyed everything....(ALSO PUBLISHED AS *CITY OF GODS*.)

OJ'S LIFE BEHIND BARS, $15.00 & $5 S/H: In 1994, Heisman Trophy winner and NFL superstar OJ Simpson was arrested for the brutal murder of his ex-wife Nicole Brown-Simpson and her friend Ron Goldman. In 1995, after the "trial of the century," he was acquitted of both murders, though most of the world believes he did it. In 2007 OJ was again arrested, but this time in Las Vegas, for armed robbery and kidnapping. On October 3, 2008 he was found guilty sentenced to 33 years and was sent to Lovelock Correctional Facility, in Lovelock, Nevada. There he met inmate-author Vernon Nelson. Vernon was granted a true, insider's perspective into the mind and life of one of the country's most notorious men; one that has never been provided...until now.

THE MOB, $16.99 & $5 S/H: PaperBoy is a Bay Area boss who has invested blood, sweat, and years into building The Mob – a network of Bay Area Street legends, block bleeders, and underground rappers who collaborate nationwide in the interest of pushing a multi-million-dollar criminal enterprise of sex, drugs, and murder.

Based on actual events, little has been known about PaperBoy, the mastermind behind The Mob, and intricate details of its operation, until now.

Follow this story to learn about some of the Bay Area underworld's most glamorous figures and famous events...

AOB, $15.00 & $5 S/H. Growing up in the Bay Area, Manny Fresh the Best had a front-row seat to some of the coldest players to ever do it. And you already know, A.O.B. is the name of the Game! So, When Manny Fresh slides through Stockton one day and sees Rosa, a stupid-bad Mexican chick with a whole lotta 'talent' behind her walking down the street tryna get some money, he knew immediately what he had to do: Put it In My Pocket!

AOB 2, $15.00 & $5 S/H.

AOB 3, $15.00 & $5 S/H.

PIMPOLOGY: THE 7 ISMS OF THE GAME, $15.00 & $5 S/H: It's been said that if you knew better, you'd do better. So, in the spirit of dropping jewels upon the rare few who truly want to know how to win, this collection of exclusive Game has been compiled. And though a lot of so-called players claim to know how the Pimp Game is supposed to go, none have revealed the real. . . Until now!

JAILHOUSE PUBLISHING FOR MONEY, POWER & FAME: $24.99 & $7 S/H: In 2010, after flirting with the idea for two years, Mike Enemigo started writing his first book. In 2014, he officially launched his publishing company, The Cell Block, with the release of five books. Of course, with no mentor(s), how-to guides, or any real resources, he was met with failure after failure as he tried to navigate the treacherous goal of publishing books from his prison cell. However, he was determined to make it. He was determined to figure it out and he refused to quit. In Mike's new book, *Jailhouse Publishing for Money, Power, and Fame*, he breaks down all his jailhouse publishing secrets and strategies, so you can do all he's done, but without the trials and tribulations he's had to go through...

KITTY KAT, ADULT ENTERTAINMENT RESOURCE BOOK, $24.99 & $7.00 S/H: This book is jam packed with hundreds of sexy non nude photos including photo spreads. The book contains the complete info on sexy photo sellers, hot magazines, page turning bookstore, sections on strip clubs, porn stars, alluring models, thought provoking stories and must-see movies.

PRISON LEGAL GUIDE, $24.99 & $7.00 S/H: The laws of the U.S. Judicial system are complex, complicated, and always growing and changing. Many prisoners spend days on end digging through its intricacies. Pile on top of the legal code the rules and regulations of a correctional facility, and you can see how high the deck is being stacked against you. Correct legal information is the key to your survival when you have run afoul of the system (or it is running afoul of you). Whether you are an accomplished jailhouse lawyer helping newbies learn the ropes, an old head fighting bare-knuckle for your rights in the courts, or a hustler just looking to beat the latest write-up – this book has something for you!

PRISON HEALTH HANDBOOK, $19.99 & $7.00 S/H: *The Prison Health Handbook* is your one-stop go-to source for information on how to maintain your best health while inside the American prison system. Filled with information, tips, and secrets from doctors, gurus, and other experts, this book will educate you on such things as proper workout and exercise regimens; yoga benefits for prisoners; how to meditate effectively; pain management tips; sensible dieting solutions; nutritional knowledge; an understanding of various cancers, diabetes, hepatitis, and other diseases all too common in prison; how to effectively deal with mental health issues such as stress, PTSD, anxiety, and depression; a list of things your doctors DON'T want YOU to know; and much, much more!

All books are available on thecellblock.net website.

You can also order by sending a money order or institutional check to:
The Cell Block; PO Box 1025; Rancho Cordova, CA 95741